ALEXANDRIA, VIRGINIA
WILLS, ADMINISTRATIONS AND GUARDIANSHIPS

1786-1800

Wesley E. Pippenger

HERITAGE BOOKS
2007

HERITAGE BOOKS
AN IMPRINT OF HERITAGE BOOKS, INC.

Books, CDs, and more—Worldwide

For our listing of thousands of titles see our website
at
www.HeritageBooks.com

Published 2007 by
HERITAGE BOOKS, INC.
Publishing Division
65 East Main Street
Westminster, Maryland 21157-5026

Copyright © 1994 Wesley E. Pippenger

All rights reserved. No part of this book may be reproduced or transmitted in any form or by any means, electronic or mechanical, including photocopying, recording or by any information storage and retrieval system without written permission from the author, except for the inclusion of brief quotations in a review.

International Standard Book Number: 978-1-58549-366-1

INTRODUCTION

By an Act of the General Assembly of Virginia, passed October 7, 1782, it was declared that *a court of hustings in the town of Alexandria, shall be, and [is] hereby constituted, [a court] of record, and as such to receive probate of wills and deeds, and grant administrations, in as full and ample manner as the county courts by law can, or may do.* Only five months previous, the court at Alexandria was granted the sole and exclusive power of granting licenses to keep ordinaries within the town, and regulating the same and restraining "tippling-houses." For the purpose this work, it is unfortunate that the probate records for the Hustings Court at Alexandria, which cover the period October 1782 to July 1786, have not been located by the compiler.

The main source for this work is the first volume of a series of court records entitled "Complete Records," which was kept by the Alexandria County Hustings Court for the period 1786 to 1800. The original of this record is found in the collection of The Library of Virginia, Archives Division, Richmond, Virginia, and is available for review on microfilm from the same institution. Additional information has been extracted from the minutes of the Hustings Court for the same period.

The following sources are used:

a. "Complete Records," Liber A, 1786-1800, pp. 1-372, original at The Library of Virginia, Archives Division, location 11/A/11/2/3.

b. Alexandria Hustings Court Minutes, 1787-1788, 1791-1793, 1791-1796, 1793-1794, 1794-1797, 1796-1797, 1798, 1798-1799, and 1800-1801. It is noted that for several of the years two different versions of the minutes exist-- one more abbreviated than the other. Few of these books have page numbers, so the date of court session is cited after the abbreviation "HCM." Though the phrasing differs between the Hustings Court minutes and the "Complete Records" Liber A text, only a few entries were found in the former which did not appear in the latter.

Of particular note is the will for Surgeon General William Brown. Dr. Brown was a son of the Reverend Richard Gustavus Brown of Port Tobacco, Maryland, and physician of the St. Andrew's Society of Alexandria. William Brown was married to Catherine Scott, and his sister Frances was married to Charles Alexander (1767-1806) of "Preston." Brown served in the Revolutionary War from 1775 to 1783, and died on January 11, 1792 in the 44th year of his age. His remains, dressed in a Continental uniform, were originally interred in the Alexander family cemetery at "Preston" plantation in Alexandria County, but were removed in 1933 to Pohick Episcopal Church cemetery, Fairfax County, Virginia.

Wesley E. Pippenger
Arlington, Virginia

ALEXANDRIA, VIRGINIA WILLS, ADMINISTRATIONS AND GUARDIANSHIPS 1786-1800

ALLISON, Mary. Will: bequeath unto my beloved niece Hannah McCasland and to her heirs all my property real and personal; leave my beloved brother Francis Allison and Daniel Roberdeau, Executors; not dated; /s/ Mary Allison; wit. Isaac S. Keith, Jemima Carson, Hugh Mittchell; proved 19 OCT 1786; pp. 4-5; Daniel Roberdeau, Philip Marsteller and William Bushby bound to justices of the Court of Hustings to take inventory, 23 FEB 1787; pp. 5-6; bond acknowledged 23 FEB 1787, p. 7.

ALLISON, William. Administrator Charles Slade; Charles Slade, John Lumsdon and Bernard Bryan, bound unto justices of the Court of Hustings for Alexandria now Sitting in the sum of $1,300 to take inventory, dated 6 AUG 1798, pp. 275-275; bond acknowledged 6 AUG 1798, pp. 276-277.

ANDERSON, Ninian. Will: of the Town of Alexandria, Biscuit Baker; all my property Real and Personal, goods and Chattels, Stock in Trade, household furniture, wearing apparel, Ready money, Book debts...to be equally devided between my brother Robert Anderson, Freeman and Baker in the City of Glasgow in the Kingdom of Scotland, North Britain, and my lawfull wife Margaret Anderson; in case of the death of my brother Robert Anderson, I will and bequeath that half of my property willed to him, to my sister Jane Haddeur of Glasgow aforesaid...in case of death of the said Jane Haddeur the said property to descend...to my sister Elizabeth Anderson of Glasgow aforesaid; constitute Robert Brocket of the Town of Alexandria aforesaid, Bricklayer, and James McClish, Cooper of Alexandria aforesaid, and Washer Blunt, Block and Pump maker of the Town aforesaid, to be my lawfull Executors; dated 8 FEB 1791; /s/ Ninian Anderson, wit. Duncan Niven, Thomas Collier and Archd. McClish, pp. 55-57; proved 22 DEC 1791, p. 57; James McClish, Robert Brocket, William Duvall and William Summers bound to justices of the Court of Hustings to take inventory, 22 DEC 1791, pp. 58-59; bond acknowledged, 22 DEC 1791, p. 59; inventory, returned 19 APR 1792, pp. 73-79.

ATKINS, Capt. Michael. Administrator William Yeaton; William Yeaton, Tobias Lear and Thomas Porter, bound unto justices of the Court of Hustings for the Town of Alexandria now Sitting and their Successors in the sum of $1,000 to take inventory,

Alexandria, Virginia Wills, Administrations and Guardianships

dated 6 AUG 1798, pp. 273-274; bond acknowledged 6 AUG 1798, p. 274; list of debts, recorded 4 FEB 1799, p. 285.

BADEN, John B. Ordered that Peggy Baden, Widow of John B. Baden deceased, be summoned to appear at the next Court to shew cause why she will not administor the said decedent's Estate. HCM, 24 FEB 1797.

BARBER, John. Administratrix Sarah Barber; Sarah Barber, Joseph Dyson and Thomas Brillatt, bound unto justices of the Court of Hustings for the Town of Alexandria, dated 1 MAY 1797, pp. 222-223; bond acknowledged 1 MAY 1797, p. 223; inventory of 26 MAY 1797, returned 5 FEB 1798, pp. 260-266; account with Sarah Barber, by Wm. Harper, Thos. Vowell, Junr. and Dennis Ramsay, recorded 5 AUG 1799, pp. 290-291.

BOA, Cavan. Administratrix Margaret Boa; Margaret Boa, Dennis Foley, Patrick Burns & Matthew Roberson, bound unto justices of the Court of Hustings for the Town of Alexandria now sitting in the sum of $3,000 to take inventory, dated 2 OCT 1798, pp. 277-278; wit. Wm. Moss; bond acknowledged, 2 OCT 1798, p. 278; appraisement, dated 4 OCT 1798, pp. 291-293; sales, dated 26 NOV 1798, pp. 293-295; account of sundry goods sold by retail previous to the commencement of Public Sale, recorded 7 OCT 1799, pp. 295-296.

BROWN, Daniel. Administrator John Limrick; John Limrick and Charles Turner, bound to justices of the Court of Hustings in the Town of Alexandria to take inventory, dated 21 NOV 1795, pp. 167-168; bond acknowledged 21 NOV 1795, p. 169.

BROWN, William. Administrator James Lawrason; James Lawrason and Charles Simms bound to justices of the Court of Hustings to take inventory, 23 FEB 1787, pp. 7-9; bond acknowledged 23 FEB 1787, p. 9.

BROWN, William. Will: **In the name of God, Amen.** I, William Brown of the Town of Alexandria in Virginia, phisician, being of sound judgment and understanding as in my ordinary stile of health, but afflicted with a disorder of uncertain event do for the more satisfactory disposition of my wordly affairs make [page 60] and ordain this as my last Will and Testament, viz.: I desire my friends to bury me without parade or expence according to the rites of the Church of England either in the burying ground at Mr. Charles Alexander's, where my child was

Alexandria, Virginia Wills, Administrations and Guardianships

buried April 28, 1785, or in the old family burying ground at "Rich Hill," in Maryland, as may be most convenient, and I desire both may be kept decently and properly inclosed, the Former at the joint expence of Mr. Alexander and me, the latter at the joint expence of Dr. Gustavus Richard Brown and me, as has been respectively agreed on between us, and I further request Mr. Charles Alexander to fullfil his engagement to me by executing and recording a proper instrument of writing for perpetuating the appropriation of the first mentioned burying ground to the use of his family and mine and their decedents for ever. As to my worldly estate it is my will and desire that during the widowhood of my wife the whole of it real and personal shall remain in her hands and under her dictation and management with the advice of my other Executors, untill my children shall respectively become entitled to the possession of their respective portions as will be hereafter particularly mentioned and described, but in case of my wife's marrying again (a step that in her circumstances it is not probable would add to her happyness, though of that she along will judge) as she would then have new and distinct interests from those of my children, it is my will and desire that from and after her marriage my other executors shall take possession and [page 61] Management of my whole estate on behalf of my children and my wife shall accept an annuity for her natural life of sixty pounds to arise as a rent charge out of my Estate and to be paid punctually unto her self for her private and seperate use and maintenance each year. The apportionment of my real Estate to be ultimately made among my children I will and desire to be as follows. To my son William the two lotts of land in the Town of Alexandria, bought of John Mills and of Messrs. Hooe and Harrison, situated on the East side of Fairfax Street with my present dwelling house, and every appurtenance belonging to the said two Lotts of Land, also to my son William one of my shares in the Potowmack Company. To my son Richard the tract of Land in Charles County, Maryland, where my late father lived, being one moiety of "Rich Hill," which moiety was bought of one Hemsley in the year 1714, by my Grandfather Dr. Gustavus Brown, and whereas there is on the North side of said "Rich Hill," a smaller piece of land called "Lomax's addition," which was also bought by my said Grandfather of one Smoot and of which the right and title is now in my eldest brother Dr. Gustavus Brown, who hath promised to convey it unto me, I do hereby request my said brother to make a Deed for the same to my son Richard as he intended and promised to do unto me. And as after such a benefice it would be improper in my Executors to make any trivial demand on behalf of my estate against my said brother Gustavus, I desire in case of his fullfilling said promise, he may not be called on for a debt due my estate of money lent him &c. in [page 62] the year 1785, also to my son Richard my other share in the Potomack Company. To my son Gustavus, the Land near "Ravensworth" in Fairfax County, Virginia where I now keep a quarter and have some Tenants, being a moiety of a tract late the property of the Revd. James Scott, and given by him to me and my wife by Deed, the other moiety of said whole trace being conveyed to Mr. Gustavus Scott of Dorsett County, Maryland, also to my son Gustavus my house and Lott in "Threlkeld's addition" to Georgetown with all the appurtenances, and whereas I have only Mr. John Threlkeld's Bond to make me a sufficient Deed for said Lott of Land, I do desire that said Deed may be forthwith obtained accordingly from Mr. Threlkeld, and I request him to makest to my son Gustavus. If after settlement of my personal Estate viz.: the payment of my debts and collection of those due to me it is found that the income of my estate is sufficient in the estimation of my Executors to support my family decently and plentifully and educate my Children, and also spare enough to purchase a third share in the Patowmack Company for my son Gustavus, I desire it may be so done, and said third share in the Patowmack Company so purchased be given to my said son Gustavus; but I do not lay this as an indispensable burden on my personal Estate, but leave it to the judgment and discretion of my Executors. To my eldest daughter Sarah the two small Lots of Land on the West side of Fairfax Street, Alexandria, which I bought of William Hunter, and whereon Alexander Perry now lives, to my two daughters Catherine and Helen, the two half Acre Lotts of Land, bordering on St. Asaph Street and [page 63] Lying between Cameron Street and Queen Street; Alexandria which I had of Mr. Charles Alexander to be divided between my said two daughters Catharine and Helen, by a line drawn through the middle of each Lott from Cameron Street to Queen Street, my daughter Catherine to have that half which borders its whole length on St. Asaph Street and wheron my Stable now Stands, and my daughter Helen to have that half which will front on Cameron Street and Queen Street only whereon a small brick dwelling

Alexandria, Virginia Wills, Administrations and Guardianships

house now stands in the tenure of Philip Ferneau, carpenter, but for the better accommodation of the latter half of said two half acre Lotts, that will belong to my daughter Helen, I will and desire that an Alley eight foot wide shall be laid off on the dividing line from Cameron Street to Queen Street (four feet on each side of said dividing line) and kept open for the use of proprietors of the Lotts on each side thereof, or in lieu of said Alley just described, two other convenient Allies of similar width, extending from St. Asaph Street to the bottom of said Lotts according as my said daughter Helen her Heirs or Assigns shall prefer Allies to be laid off in the one manner or in the other, but my daughter Catherine her Heirs or Assigns may at anytime require said option to be made, and if not made within three months thereafter, may proceed to lay of said Alley or allies in either of the ways above described and when the same shall have been once so laid off they shall not be subject to alterations except by mutual concent. And whereas my military bounty of Lands on the waters of the Ohio, committed to the charge of Colo. John Campbell of Luisville at the falls of the Ohio to be by [page 64] him located and surveyed (he to have one fourth thereof for his trouble by agreement) have not yet been all surveyed as I know of, but when surveyed will consist of five surveys of twelve hundred acres each, I allot the same to my several Children as follows-- The first survey of which I have some time since had the patent situated at the conflux of the Rivers Cumberland and Ohio, and which was by Lott drawn to be first located of all the military lands in that Country and which Land containing 1,200 acres extends along and bounds on both rivers Cumberland and Ohio, I give to my son Gustavus, I also give my said son Gustavus a small tract of one hundred Acres situated not far distant from the above of which I also have the patent made out in my name but the right whereof or warrant of Survey I had of David Crawley a soldier or which was surveyed along with seven hundred acres more, under soldier's rights that were drawn unto Lott No. 6 (as I have been informed) for priority of location, my other four surveys consisting of twelve hundred acres each whereof I have yet received no returns, from Col. Campbell my agent but which I expect will be located higher up the Ohio between the Rivers Sciota and Miami, on the northwestern side of the Ohio, these I give to my four Children, Sarah, Richard, Catherine and Helen, one of said surveys of 1,200 acres each unto each of my said four Children last named, they to choose each his

Alexandria, Virginia Wills, Administrations and Guardianships

or her portion as soon as the same shall be surveyed and patented, and as they shall respectively come of full age according to seniority. To my son William, I give no land in the Western Country, because [page 65] his Grandfather the Revd. James Scott hath by his Will given him some which he holds in joint tenancy with Mr. Gustavus Scott son of said Revd. James Scott. And whereas I have upwards of two thousand one hundred pounds in Military Certificates of the State of Virginia bearing an annual Interest of six percent at present payable by said State. I will and desire that the whole sum of my said military Certificates be equally divided among my three daughters, Sarah, Catherine, and Helen, each to be entitled to receive Five hundred pounds thereof on her arrival at the age of nineteen years or on her marriage, and the residue of Six hundred and odd pounds to remain in the hands of my wife during her life and widdowhood, in order for her to receive annually the interest accrueing thereon to assist in the support of her household, but the said six hundred and odd pounds in military Certificates shall be considered also as a part of the portion of my daughters and on the death or second marriage of my wife shall also be divided equally among them, viz.: my three daughters, Sarah, Catherine, and Helen, I give also to my son Gustavus half a Lott of Ground in the Town of Bath in Berkley County, No. (39) according to the plan of the said Town, which half Lott I had of Mathew Whiting, Esquire, the Deed of Conveyance is among the papers of the Clerk's Office of the General Court of Virginia, where it hath been proved by two Witnesses, and remains to be proved by Mr. Thomas Whiting the third witness, who is requested to prove it the first oportunity [sic] in [page 66] order that it may be duly recorded and the Original Deed received from the office. I appoint for my Executors to see this my last will duly accomplished and carried into effect, My wife Mrs. Catherine Brown (but to be disqualified from acting as my Executrix in case of her making a second marriage) my old friend and Uncle Dr. Gustavus Richard Brown of Charles County in Maryland, and my Good and worthy friends Bushrod Washington, George Gilpin, William Herbert, and Richard Conway, Esquires, all of Alexandria, and I request they will not decline acting as many of them as can make it convenient hoping that through the prudence and discretion and Economical industrious turn of my wife they will have little trouble therewith except in advising her and supporting her by their counterance and authority. I

Alexandria, Virginia Wills, Administrations and Guardianships

desire that all debts due to me may be spedily collected, and that Mr. James Russell or some one of similar integrity and industry be employed to do it, and as some of my accounts (that arose in the more hurried part of my business) are kept in a more abbreviated manner than is usual, I request my friend Mr. Wilson Compton who is well acquainted therewith to assist or instruct the Collector that shall be employed in drawing them off in the usual form, the debts that I owe will of course be paid, and I hope the collections made, or at any rate those with the Interest accumulating and accruing from my Military Certificates will answer to pay in seasonable time all I owe, without the alienation of any of my other pursonal Estate for that purpose. I desire that my negroes, Stocks [page 67] moveables, money and other personal property may remain undivided either in the hands of my wife during her widowhood or in case of her death or second marriage, in the hands of my other Executors, to be by them nurtured and applied to the best advantage untill the first of my Children shall arrive at full age, and then an equal division of the whole thereof to be made by my Executors among all my Children, each of whom on arriving at full age, shall be entitled to receive into their own possession respectively only half their share of either real or personal Estate herein bequeathed them respectively, unless my wife shall then be either dead or married a second time, in which case each child shall receive into possession his or her full portion of both real or personal Estate, my sons on arriving at the age of twenty one and my Daughters at the age of nineteen years or at their marriage respectively, or unless my wife being still alive and remaining a widow, and in possession of the rest of my estate (as above directed) shall choose to give up to any child the whole of his or her portion but my wife shall have a right during her natural life and widowhood to retain in her possession if she so chooses one half the portion of both real and personal Estate herein allotted to each child; and where a child is come of age and any part of his or her porition is not capable of Division (such as a plantation or house and Lott or the like) in such case either party (viz.: my wife and child unto whom it is bequeathed) may pay unto the other party [page 68] half the annual value or rent thereof according as they may agree, and by so doing, possess and occupy the whole or if they cannot agree as to the sum that one half of such property is worth by the year, then it shall be ascertained by my other acting Executors. And my wife shall have the option of either to give possession of such property to such child and receive the annual half rent thereof or to retain it in her own possession and pay such child such annual half rent provided however that in no case shall such dues from mother to child or from child to mother accumulate beyond one year but if not demanded when due and before a second years half rent shall become due, all except the last shall be considered as relinquished and not afterwards claimed. In case of my wife's marrying a second time my will and desire is, and I hereby direct that my other Executors immediately take into their possession and charge on behalf of my children the whole of my Estate real and personal, and as each child shall arrive sons at the age of twenty one, and daughters at the age of nineteen years give unto each in possession the whole that is herein bequeathed to them, respectively, but in this case each childs portion shall be burdened as follows in order to raise the sum of Sixty pounds annually during the natural life of my wife, to be paid to her for her private and particular use and maintenance, viz.: The real estate bequeathed to each of my sons shall be burdened with the payment of twelve pounds annually to my wife which shall be as a rent chargeable thereon, and liable to be distressed for, and the interest accrueing on the Military Certificates bequeathed to my daughters (which in the case of my wife's second [page 69] marriage and consequent relinquishment of all claim and possession of every part of my Estate except the said annuity of sixty pounds, will be upwards of seven hundred pounds, unto each of my daughters) the said interest shall be chargeable with the payment of eight pounds Annually to my wife, on behalf and account of each of my daughters, so as in the whole to make up the sum of sixty pounds pr. annum for the use of my wife to be paid her for her Special maintenance, but in this case also the said annual sum due to my wife shall not be suffered to accumulate beyond a single year, and if she do not claim the payment thereof each year when it becomes due, and before the annuity of the Succeeding year shall become due all former claims on this score except for one and the last year shall be considered to have been voluntarily relinquished by her and shall not afterwards be claimed by or on her behalf. I will and desire that my Executors sell of to the last advantage my stock of medicines and shop furniture and my library and such other articles of movable effects as they may judge to be of a perishable nature and not necessary for the immediate use and accommodation of my family, and whereas I am just entering into a partnership with Dr. Gustavus B. Campbell for carrying on the practice of Phisick and business of selling drugs, if Dr. Campbell will purchase the whole stock on hand at the rate of sixty pr. Cent on the Sterling cost (which are the terms on which I purpose letting him have half the present stock in order to [page 70] his becoming a partner) and will give good security for the payment, I desire in such case the whole stock of medicines and shop furniture may be sold to him (as they stand) on those terms, otherwise I desire they may be divided into small parcels of each article (so as to suit private practitioners of Phisic) and after being duly advertised, sold off at publick sale in such manner as my Executors shall judge to be most advantageous. In case of claims coming against my Estate after my decease, I believe my books of accompts area good Criterion of their authenticity, and I would therefore have my Executors to suspect all such to be fictitious and unjust as are not found to correspond with my books for I believe these to be accurately and fairly kept, and contain, as well, an acocunt of what I owe, as of what is owing unto me, to obviate claims that are unjust. I have put away certain bundles of receipts and bills arranged according to the respective years in which the transactions happened in seperate parcels for several years back, and the respective year is marked on each, in order to prevent contests among those I leave behind me, and who will be interested in my Estate. I hereby will and direct that in case of any dispute concerning the true meaning and intention of any part of this my last will and Testament, arising amont those to whom I have bequeathed any thing or any of them, a statement of the matter in dispute shall be made in writing by each party concerned in the dispute and submitted to Bushrod Washington, Esqr., to be by him determined or if a decision by him cannot be obtained it shall in like manner be [page 71] submitted to any one Judge of the General or District Courts of Virginia whose opinion thereon can be obtained, and such determination of the Interpretation and intention of this my last Will and Testament so made by either and given under their hands respectively shall be final and decisive between the parties, under penalty of such as shall refuse to submit to and acquiesce under such decision, forfeiting all claim and title with respect to the subject or matter in dispute, derived from the Will and Testament. Lastly, I declare the above written in my own hand, and contained on this and nine preceding pages to be my last Will and Testament and hereby ratify it as such by subscribing my name and affixing my Seal.

W. Brown [seal]

Witnesses: Gusts. B. Campbell, Ja: Russell, Robt. Mainning, and John Steuart.

This is a Codicil to the above last Will and Testament of me William Brown which is to be added to and made part of the same. Whereas in my aforesaid Last Will and Testament the Legacies and bequests made to my son William Brown are absolute and I have upon reflection thought that it may tend to secure the good behaviour of my said son, and to prevent him from runing into that dissipation and extravagance into which he may be led by possessing his fortune absolutely at any particular period, now I do hereby will and desire that the Legacies and bequests made to my said son [page 72] may be retained by my Executors in their hands and not delivered to my said son, untill by the good conduct of my said son my wife and my Executors Doctor Gustavus Richard Brown and Bushrod Washington shall think it proper that the same or any part thereof should be delivered into his possession, my said son having a competent allowance thereout for his maintenance at the discretion of said wife and Executors Doctor Gustavus Richard Brown and Bushrod Washington, and if my said son should by ill conduct prove himself unfit in the opinion of my wife and said two Executors to possess his estate herein before bequeathed, or if my said son should dispose of the contingent interest herein before bequeathed, the possession of which is suspended as above, before he is put into possession thereof by my said Executors, then and in such case I desire that whatever I have herein before given him may be equally divided amongst my other children and their Heirs, my intention is to restrain my said son from dissipating his Estate by keeping it out of his possession untill my wife and said two Executors may find in him a disposition to use it with prudence. In Witness whereof I have to this writing (which I declare to be a Codicil to my said last Will and Testament and as part thereof) set my hand and seal this 24th day of November 1791. Signed Sealed & published by the said William Brown as and for a Codicil, to be added to and be part of his last Will and Testament in presence of us who have subscribed our names in his presence & at his request, Peter Wise, Junior, Charles Alexander, and Gusts. B. Campbell.

W. Brown.

Alexandria, Virginia Wills, Administrations and Guardianships

Proved at a Court of Hustings held for the Town of Alexandria, 23d of February 1792, p. 73; Catharine Brown, John Fitzgerald and James Keith, bound to justices of the Court of Hustings to take inventory, 23 FEB 1792, pp. 79-80; bond acknowledged, 23 FEB 1792, p. 80; inventory, pp. 85-89, inventory of the library, instruments, &c., by Jonah Thompson, James Kennedy and Thos. Porter, pp. 89-107; inventory and appraisement returned and recorded 22 NOV 1792, p. 108; one half of the Medicine &c. remaining in the Shop of Messrs. Brown & Campbell at the decease of Dr. Wm. Brown, July 14th, 1792, pp. 109-114; shop furniture &c., pp. 115-116.

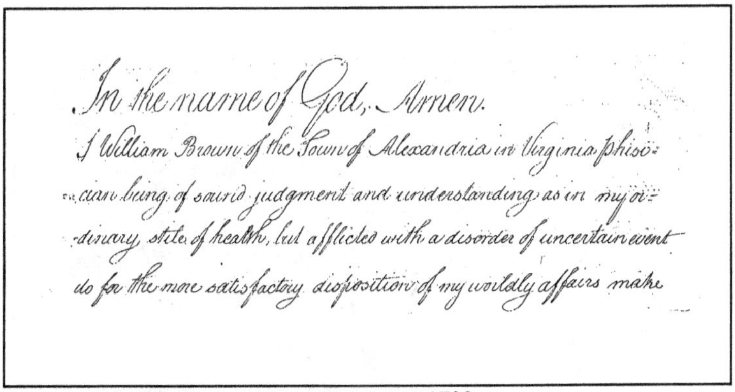

Figure 1 - Will of Dr. William Brown, d. 1792.

and ordain this as my last Will and Testament Viz.
I desire my friends to bury me without parade or expence according to
the rites of the Church of England either in the burying ground at Mr
Charles Alexanders, where my child was buried April 28. 1785. or
in the old family burying ground at Rich Hill in Maryland as may
be most convenient, and I desire both may be kept decently and
properly inclosed; the former at the joint expence of Mr Alexander and
me, the latter at the joint expence of Dr Gustavus Richard Brown
and me, as has been respectively agreed on between us, and I further
request Mr Charles Alexander to fullfil his engagement to me by
executing and recording a proper instrument of Writing, for perpetuating the appropriation of the first mentioned burying ground
to the use of his family and mine and their decendants for ever.
As to my worldly estate it is my will and desire that during the
widowhood of my wife the whole of it real and personal shall remain in her hands and under her direction and management
with the advice of my other executors, untill my children shall respectively become entitled to the possession of their respective portions as
will be hereafter particularly mentioned and described, but in case
of my wife's marrying again (a step that in her circumstances
it is not probable would add to her happyness, though of that she
alone will judge) as she would then have new and distinct interests
from those of my children, it is my will and desire that from and
after her marriage my other executors shall take possession and

Management of my whole estate on behalf of my children, and my wife shall accept an annuity for her natural life of sixty pounds to arise as a rentcharge out of my Estate and to be paid punctually unto her self for her private and seperate use and maintenance each year. The apportionment of my real Estate to be ultimately made among my children I will and desire to be as follows. To my son William the two Lotts of land in the Town of Alexandria, bought of John Mills and of Messrs. Hooe and Harrison, situated on the East side of Fairfax Street with my present dwelling house, and every appurtenance belonging to the said two Lotts of Land, also to my son William one of my shares in the Potowmack Company. To my son Richard the tract of Land in Charles County, Maryland, where my late father lived, being one moiety of Rich Hill, which moiety was bought of one Hemsley in the year 1714. by my Grandfather Dr. Gustavus Brown; and whereas there is on the North side of said Rich Hill a smaller piece of land called Somas's addition, which was also bought by my said Grandfather of one Smoot, and of which the right and title is now in my eldest brother Dr. Gustavus Brown, who hath promised to convey it unto me, I do hereby request my said brother to make a Deed for the same to my son Richard as he intended and promised to do unto me. And as after such a benefice it would be improper in my Executors to make any trivial demand on behalf of my estate against my said brother Gustavus, I desire in case of his fullfilling said promise, he may not be called on for a debt due my estate, of money lent him &c. in the year 1785. also to my son Richard my other share in the Potow-mack Company. To my son Gustavus the Land near Ravensworth in Fairfax County Virginia where I now keep a quarter and have some Tenants, being a moiety of a tract late the property of the Rev.d James Scott, and given by him to me and my wife by Deed, the other moiety of said whole tract being conveyed to Mr. Gustavus Scott of Dorsett County Maryland, also to my son Gustavus my house and Lott in Threlkeld's addition to Georgetown with all the appurtenances, and whereas I have only Mr. John Threlkeld's Bond to make me a sufficient Deed for said Lott of Land, I do desire that said Deed may be forthwith obtained accordingly from Mr. Threlkeld, and I request him to make it to my son Gustavus, If after settlement of my personal Estate Viz. the payment of my debts and collection of those due to me it is found that the income of my estate is sufficient in the estima- tion of my Executors to support my family decently and plentifully and educate my Children, and also spare enough to purchase a third share in the Patowmack Company for my son Gustavus, I desire it may be so done, and said third share in the Patowmack Company so purchased be given to my said son Gustavus; but I do not lay this as an indispensable burden on my personal Estate, but leave it to the judgment and discretion of my Executors. To my eldest daughter Sarah the two small Lots of Land on the west side of Fairfax Street Alexandria, which I bought of William Hunter, and whereon Alex- ander Perry now lives. To my two daughters Catherine and Helen, the two half Acre Lotts of Land, bordering on St. Asaph Street and lying between Cameron Street and Queen Street, Alexandria which I had of Mr. Charles Alexander to be divided between my said two daughters Catharine and Helen, by a line drawn through the middle of each Lott from Cameron Street to Queen Street, my daughter Catherine to have that half which borders its whole length on St Asaph Street and whereon my Stable now stands, and my daughter Helen to have that half which will front on Cameron Street and Queen Street only, whereon a small brick dwelling house now stands in the tenure of Philip Terneau carpenter, but for the better accommodation of the latter half of said two half acre Lotts, that will belong to my daughter Helen, I will and desire that an Alley eight foot wide shall be laid off on the dividing line from Cameron Street to Queen Street (four feet on each side of said dividing line) and kept open for the use of the proprietors of the Lotts on each side thereof, or in lieu of said Alley just described, two other convenient Alleys of similar width, extending from St Asaph Street to the bottom of said Lotts according as my said daughter Helen her Heirs or Assigns shall prefer Alleys to be laid off in the one manner or in the other, but my daughter Catherine her Heirs or Assigns may at any time require said option to be made, and if not made within three months thereafter, may proceed to lay off said Alley or allies in either of the ways above described, and when the same shall have been once so laid off they shall not be subject to alterations except by mutual consent. And, whereas my military bounty of Lands on the waters of the Ohio, committed to the charge of Col.º John Campbell of Louisville at the falls of Ohio to be by

RUM, located and surveyed, (he to have one fourth thereof for his trouble by agreement) have not yet been all surveyed as I know of, but when surveyed will consist of five surveys of twelve hundred acres each. I allot the same to my several Children as follows —
The first survey of which I have some time since had the patent situated at the conflux of the Rivers Cumberland and Ohio, and which was by Lott drawn to be first located of all the military lands in that Country, and which land containing 1200 acres extends along and bounds on both rivers Cumberland and Ohio, I give to my son Gustavus. I also give my said son Gustavus a small tract of one hundred Acres situated not far distant from the above of which I also have the patent made out in my name but the right whereof or warrant of Survey I had of David Crawley a soldier or which was surveyed along with seven hundred acres more, under soldier's rights that were drawn unto Lott N°. 6 (as I have been informed) for priority of location, my other four surveys consisting of twelve hundred acres each, whereof I have yet received no returns, from Col: Camp=bell my agent but which I expect will be located higher up the Ohio, between the Rivers Scioto and Miami, on the northwestern side of the Ohio, these I give to my four Children, Sarah, Richard, Cathe=rine, and Helen, one of said surveys of 1200 acres each unto each of my said four Children last named, they to choose each his or her portion as soon as the same shall be surveyed and patented, and as they shall respectively come of full age according to seniority. To my son William I give no land in the Western Country, because

his Grandfather the rev.d James Scott hath by his will given him some which he holds in joint tenancy with Mr Gustavus Scott son of said Rev.d James Scott. And whereas I have upwards of two thousand one hundred pounds in Military Certificates of the State of Virginia bearing an annual Interest of six percent at present payable by said State, I will and desire that the whole sum of my said military Certificates be equally divided among my three daughters Sarah, Catherine, and Helen, each to be entitled to receive Five hundred pounds thereof on her arrival at the age of nineteen years, or on her marriage, and the residue of Six hundred and odd pounds to remain in the hands of my wife during her life and widowhood, in order for her to receive annually the interest accrueing thereon, to assist in the support of her household, but the said six hundred and odd pounds in military Certificates shall be considered also as a part of the portion of my daughters and on the death or second marriage of my wife shall also be divided equally among them viz: my three daughters Sarah, Catherine, and Helen, I give also to my son Gustavus half a Lott of Ground in the Town of Bath in Berkley County N: (34) according to the plan of the said Town, which half Lott I had of Mathew Whiting Esquire, the Deed of Conveyance is among the papers of the Clerks Office of the General Court of Virginia, where it hath been proved by two Witnesses, and remains to be proved by Mr. Thomas Whiting the third witness, who is requested to prove it the first oportunity in

Order that it may be duly recorded and the Original Deed received from the Office. I appoint for my Executors to see this my last will duly accomplished and carried into effect, My wife Mrs. Catherine Brown (but to be disqualified from acting as my Executrix in case of her making a second marriage) my old friend and Uncle Dr. Gustavus Richard Brown of Charles County in Maryland, and my good and worthy friends Bushrod Washington, George Gilpin, William Herbert, and Richard Conway, Esquires all of Alexandria, and I request they will not decline acting, as many of them as can make it convenient, hoping that through the prudence and discretion and economical industrious turn of my wife they will have little trouble therewith except in advising her and supporting her by their countenance and authority. I desire that all debts due to me may be speedily collected, and that Mr. James Russell or some one of similar integrity and industry be employed to do it, and as some of my accounts (that arose in the more hurried part of my business) are kept in a more abbreviated manner than is usual, I request my friend Dr. Wilson Crompton who is well acquainted therewith to assist or instruct the Collector that shall be employed in drawing them off in the usual form, the debts that I owe will of course be paid, and I hope the collections made, or at any rate those with the Interest accumulating and accrueing from my Military Certificates will answer to pay in seasonable time all I owe, without the alienation of any of my other personal Estate for that purpose. I desire that my negroes, stocks,

in Cash & money and other personal property, may remain undivided either in the hands of my wife during her widowhood or
in case of her death or second marriage, in the hands of my other
Executors to be by them nurtured and applied to the best advantage
until the first of my Children shall arrive at full age, and then
an equal division of the whole thereof to be made by my Executors
among all my Children, each of whom on arriving at full age
shall be intitled to receive into their own possession respectively
only half their share of either real or personal Estate herein bequeathed them respectively; unless my wife shall then be either
dead or married a second time; in which case each child shall
receive into possession his or her full portion of both real or personal
Estate, my sons on arriving at the age of twenty one and my
Daughters at the age of nineteen years or at their marriage respectively; or unless my wife being still alive and remaining a widow and in possession of the rest of my estate (as above directed)
shall choose to give up to any child the whole of his or her portion
But my wife shall have a right during her natural life and
widowhood to retain in her possession, if she so chooses one half
the portion of both real and personal Estate herein allotted to each
child; and where a child is come of age and any part of his or her
portion is not capable of Division (such as a plantation or house
and Lot or the like) in such case either party (viz: my wife and
children to whom it is bequeathed) may pay unto the other party

half the annual value or rent thereof according as they may agree, and by so doing, possess and occupy the whole, or if they cannot agree as to the sum that one half such property is worth by the year, then it shall be ascertained by my other acting Executors. And my wife shall have the option either to give possession of such property to such child and receive the annual half rent thereof, or to retain it in her own possession and pay such child such annual half rent, provided however that in no case shall such sues from mother to child or from child to mother accumulate beyond one year, but if not demanded when due and before a second years half rent shall become due, all except the last shall be considered as relinquished and not afterwards claimed. In case of my wifes marrying a second time my will and desire is, and I hereby direct that my other Executors immediately take into their possession and charge on behalf of my children the whole of my Estate real and personal; and as each child shall arrive sons at the age of twenty one, and daughters at the age of nineteen years give unto each in possession the whole that is herein bequeathed to them respectively, but in this case each childs portion shall be burdened as follows in order to raise the sum of sixty pounds annually during the natural life of my wife, to be paid to her for her private and particular use and maintenance. Viz. The real Estate bequeathed to each of my sons shall be burdened with the payment of twelve pounds annually, to my wife which shall be as a rent chargeable thereon, and liable to be distressed for, and the interest accrueing on the Military Certificates bequeathed to my daughters (which in the case of my wifes second marriage and consequent relinquishment of all claim and possession of every part of my Estate, except the said annuity of sixty pounds, will be upwards of seven hundred pounds, unto each, of my daughters) the said interest shall be chargeable with the payment of eight pounds Annually to my wife, on behalf and account of each of my daughters, so as in the whole to make up the sum of sixty pounds per annum for the use of my wife to be paid her for her Special maintenance, but in this case also the said annual sum due to my wife shall not be suffered to accumulate beyond a single year, and if she do not claim the payment thereof, each year when it becomes due, and before the annuity of the succeeding year shall become due all former claims on this score, except for one and the last year, shall be considered to have been voluntarily relinquished by her and shall not afterwards be claimed by or on her behalf, I will and desire that my Executors sell of to the best advantage my stock of medicines and shop furniture and my library and such other articles of movable effects as they may judge to be of a perishable nature and not necessary for the immediate use and accommodation of my family, and whereas I am just entering into a partnership with Dr. Gustavus R. Campbell for carrying on the practice of Phisick and business of selling drugs, if Dr. Campbell will purchase the whole stock on hand at the rate of sixty per Cent on the Sterling cost (which are the terms on which I purpose letting him have half the present stock in accounts his becoming a partner) and will give good security for the pay-ment. I desire in such case the whole stock of medecines and Shop furniture may be sold to him (as they stand) on those terms, other-wise I desire they may be divided into small parcels of each article (so as to suit private practitioners of Phisic) and after being duly advertized, sold off at publick sale in such manner as my Execu-tors shall judge to be most advantageous. In case of claims coming against my Estate after my decease, I believe my books of accompts are a good Criterion of their authenticity, and I would therefore have my Executors to suspect all such to be fictitious and unjust as are not found to correspond with my books for I believe these to be accu-rately and fairly kept, and contain, as well, an account of what I owe, as of what is owing unto me, to obviate claims that are unjust I have put away certain bundles of receipts and bills arranged according to the respective years in which the transactions hap-pened in seperate parcels for several years back, and the respec-tive year is marked on each, in order to prevent contests among those I leave behind me, and who will be interested in my Estate I hereby will and direct that in case of any dispute concerning the true meaning and intention of any part of this my last will and Testament, arising among those to whom I have bequeathed any thing, or any of them, a statement of the matter in dispute shall be made in writing by each party concerned in the dispute and submitted to Bushrod Washington Esqr to be by him determined or if a decision by him cannot be obtained it shall in like manner be

Submitted to any one Judge of the General or District Courts of Virginia whose opinion thereon can be obtained, and such determination of the Interpretation and intention of this my last Will and Testament so made by either and given under their hands respectively shall be final and decisive between the parties, under penalty of such as shall refuse to submit to and acquiesce under such decision, forfeiting all claim and title with respect to the subject or matter in dispute derived from the Will and Testament. Lastly I declare the above written in my own hand, and contained on this and nine preceding pages to be my last Will and Testament and hereby ratify it as such by subscribing my name and affixing my Seal.

Witness — W. Brown (Seal)

Gust.º B. Campbell
Ja: Russell
Rob.t Manning
John Stewart

This is a Codicil to the above last Will and Testament of me William Brown which is to be added to and made part of the same. Whereas in my aforesaid Last Will and Testament the Legacies and bequests made to my son William Brown are absolute and I have upon reflection thought that it may tend to secure the good behaviour of my said son, and to prevent him from running into that dissipation and extravagance into which he may be led by possessing his fortune absolutely at any particular period. Now I do hereby will and desire that the Legacies and bequests made to my said son

MAY be retained by my Executors in their hands and not delivered to my said son, untill by the good conduct of my said son my wife and my Executors Doctor Gustavus Richard Brown and Bushrod Washington shall think it proper that the same or any part thereof should be delivered into his possession, my said son having a competent allowance thereout for his maintenance at the discretion of said wife and Executors Doctor Gustavus Richard Brown and Bushrod Washington, and if my said son should by ill conduct prove himself unfit in the opinion of my wife and said two Executors to possess his estate herein before bequeathed, or if my said son should dispose of the contingent interest herein before bequeathed, the possession of which is suspended as above, before he is put into possession thereof, by my said Executors, then and in such case I desire that whatever I have herein before given him may be equally divided amongst my other children and their Heirs, my intention is to restrain my said son from dissipating his Estate by keeping it out of his possession untill my wife and said two Executors may find in him a disposition to use it with prudence.

In Witness whereof I have to this writing (which I declare to be a Codicil to my said last Will and Testament and as part thereof) set my hand and seal this 24th day of November 1791.

Signed Sealed & published by the said William Brown as and for a Codicil, to be added to and be part of his last Will and Testament in presence of us who have subscribed our names in his presence & at his request

W. Brown (Seal)

Peter Wise Junior
Charles Alexander
Gust.s B. Campbell

> At a Court of Hustings held for the Town of Alexandria 23 of February 1792. The last Will and Testament of William Brown deceased was presented in Court by Catherine Brown Executrix therein named who made oath thereto, and the same being proved by the oath of Charles Simms, George Gilpin, and James Keith to be wholly writ by the said Testator, is together with a Codicil thereto annexed which was proved by the oath of Charles Alexander and Peter Wise Jr to be the act and Deed of the said Testator, ordered to be recorded And the said Executrix having performed what the Laws require a Certificate is granted her for obtaining a probate thereof in due form.

BROWN, Windsor. Administrator James Davenport; James Davenport and John Wise, bound unto justices of the Court of Hustings in the Town of Alexandria for $8,000 to take inventory, dated 2 MAY 1797, pp. 227-229; bond acknowledged, 2 MAY 1797, p. 230.

BURNETT, Sarah, George Burnett and Charles Burnett, wards of Michael Gretter; Michael Gretter and Jacob Shuck bound to gentlemen of the Court of Hustings, 22 FEB 1793, pp. 124-125; bond acknowledged 22 FEB 1793, p. 125.

BUTT, Adam. Administrator Jacob Butt; Jacob Butt, John Boyer and Michael Steiber, bound to justices of the Court of Hustings in Alexandria to take inventory, 23 JAN 1794, pp. 133-134; bond acknowledged, 23 JAN 1794, p. 134; inventory by George Coryell, Adam S. Swope, Christian Slimmer and Jacob Shuck, dated 13 FEB 1794, pp. 142-143; recorded 24 MAY 1794, p. 143.

Alexandria, Virginia Wills, Administrations and Guardianships

BUTTS, Jacob. Administrators Daniel Curtain and Thomas Murray; Thomas Murray, John Sullivan and Dennis Foley, bound to justices of the Court of Hustings in the Town of Alexandria to take inventory, dated 25 SEP 1795, pp. 164-164; bond acknowledged 25 SEP 1795, p. 165.

BUTTS, Jacob, orphan of Adam Butts, deceased, ward of John Boyer; John Boyer, Abraham Faw and Philip Marsteller, bound to justices of the Court of Hustings for the Town of Alexandria, dated 21 OCT 1796, pp. 207-208; bond acknowledged, 21 OCT 1796, p. 209.

CHAPMAN, William. Administrator John Foster; John Foster, James Bacon and George Gilpin, bound unto Amos Alexander, George Taylor, George Slacum and Charles Alexander, Junr. in the just and full sum of $3,000 to take inventory, dated 6 DEC 1800, pp. 329-330, wit. Wm. Moss and G. Deneale; bond acknowledged 6 DEC 1800, p. 335.

COPPER, Elizabeth. Will: of the Town of Alexandria, County of Fairfax...; after funeral expences, to my dear children named Nancy Copper, Samuel Copper, Sarah Copper, Elizabeth Copper, all my Household furniture to be equally divided; to my eldest Daughter my cow; desire that my daughters shall remain in my dwelling house where I now dwell; ordain William Duvall and Robert Lyle as executors; dated 20 APR 1789; /s/ Eliza. Copper; wit. Jno. C. Kempff, Andrew Reintzell, Richard Weightman and Casina Lake; proved 22 APR 1790; pp. 18-19; Robert Brockett, William Ward and William Summers, bound to justices of the Court of Hustings to take inventory, 22 APR 1790, pp. 19-20; bond acknowledged, 22 APR 1790, p. 20; inventory by John Longdon, Robert Lyle and Roger Chew, pp. 20-22, styled Elizabeth "Cooper;" account of sales, 3 MAY 1790, filed 25 JUL 1790, pp. 22-23; account for Elizabeth "Cooper," by William Ward and Robert Brockett, recorded 24 OCT 1794, pp. 143-144.

CRAIK, James, Junr. Administrator James Craik; James Craik and James Kennedy, bound to justices of the Court of Hustings in the Town of Alexandria to take inventory, dated 25 SEP 1795, pp. 166-167; bond acknowledged, 25 SEP 1795, p. 167.

CROUCHER, Thomas. Administrator William Cock; William Cock and Willoughby Tibbs, bound to justices of the Court of Hustings to take inventory, 23 JUN 1791, pp. 39-40; bond acknowledged 23 JUN 1791, p. 41; inventory by James Caverly,

Alexandria, Virginia Wills, Administrations and Guardianships

Lewis Weston and Michael Thorn, dated 1 OCT 1791, returned 23 JAN 1794, p. 130.

CURTAIN, Daniel. Will: ...of the Town of Alexandria; to my son William Curtain upon his arrival at the age of twenty one years, and to his heirs and assigns for ever a part or dividend of ground situate lying and being on the South side of Duke Street with all the houses and appurtenances late in the occupation of [blank] Kyger, Tanner, the said Ground to begin on the said south side of Duke Street at a ten foot alley and the west side of the alley and to run westerly with Duke Street twenty six feet and so Southerly that number of feet in width Southerly to another ten foot alley to run across my Ground on Duke Street, through the middle of the lot, the first mentioned alley to run north and South and the dwelling house stands on the West side thereof; unto my said son William Curtain...upon his arrival at the age of twenty one years all the Ground I hold on the east side of the said last described alley on Duke Street and to run Southerly with its width to the said other mentioned alley, but it is my will & desire that if my said son dies without heirs by marriage that any Estate given him by those two bequests shall become the property of all my other children equally and their heirs...; all my said other children whose names are Elizabeth, Catharine and Elenor; unto my said Daughter Elizabeth Curtain...all that part of my said lott of ground which lies to the westward (on Duke Street) of the part first devised to my said son, and to run Southerly with its width to the said cross alley, upon the same terms and under the same restrictions of the parts devised to my said son; unto my said two daughters Catharine and Elenor...all the rest and residue of my said lott of ground, which lies to the Southward of the said cross alley, to be equally divided between them by my Executors or any person...; reserving to my wife Susanna Curtain her right of Dower of and in the said lott of ground; all the money I have now by me which is about four hundred and thirty Dollars in bank notes to Interest or purchase bank Stock with and make equal divisions thereof between my wife and children, and that they apply any money arising from the sale of such of my personal estate as they think necessary to sell; appoint my Friends, Amos Alexander and William Hartshorne, Junr., Executors...and guardians to my children and it is my will and desire that my said Executors and Guardians to my children do educate them as well as my Estate on the Profits thereof will admit of that at the age of sixteen years they do bind my said son to learn the trade of a cooper till he arrives at the age of twenty one years; dated 23 DEC 1799, /s/ Daniel Curtain; wit. Cleon Moore, Arcd. McClish, and John Reardon, pp. 309-312; proved 3 MAR 1800, p. 312; Amos Alexander, William Hartshorne, Junr., Charles Turner, Richard Lewis and Mordecai Miller, bound to justices of the Court of Hustings for the Town of Alexandria now sitting in the sum of $1,100 to take inventory, dated 3 MAR 1800, pp. 312-313; bond acknowledged 3 MAR 1800, pp. 313-314.

CURTZ, Nicholas. On Motion of Peter Wise, it is ordered that the Serjeant of this Corporation do take into his possession all the Estate of Nicholas Curtz, deceased, and that he administer the same as the Law directs first satisfying a Judgment and Costs obtained against the deceased by Adam Ebert. HCM, 19 FEB 1796, p. 317.

DAVIS, Samuel. Will: ...of the Town of Alexandria; ...unto my Wife Mary all my household and Kitchen furniture and p[ink spot]e to have unto her and her Executors and Administrators for ever; all the rest and residue of my Estate both real and personal unto my said Wife Mary & my four Children Joseph, Sarah, Mary and Hannah and Ann, and to their Heirs...to be divided equally among them; appoint my said Wife Mary Executrix and my friends William Harper, Abram Hewes Executors...and guardians of my said children; dated 29 AUG 1798, /s/ Saml. Davis; wit. Jas. Keith, John Reynolds, Isaac Gibson and Benjm. Shreve; proved 8 MAY 1795, pp. 268-269; Mary Davis, Wm. Harper, Abram Hewes, Benjamin Shreve, Chas. Harper & Aaron Hewes, bound unto justices of the Court of Hustings for the Town of Alexandria in the sum of $10,000 to take inventory, 8 MAY 1798, pp. 269-270; bond acknowledged, 8 MAY 1798, p. 270.

DEEBLE, William. Administrator John Duffy; John Duffy and Charles Slade, bound to justices of the Court of Hustings in the Town of Alexandria, dated 21 MAY 1796, pp. 183-184; bond acknowledged, 21 MAY 1796, p. 185.

DEWER, George. Administrator William Rickard; Wm. Rickard and Charles Jones, bound to justices of the Court of Hustings for the Town of Alexandria, dated 23 DEC 1796, pp. 212-215; bond acknowledged 23 DEC 1796, pp. 215-216.

DICK, Archibald and Julia Dick, wards of Elisha Cullen Dick; Elisha Cullen Dick and James McRea, bound to

Alexandria, Virginia Wills, Administrations and Guardianships

justices of the Court of Hustings in Alexandria for guardianship, dated 3 AUG 1796, p. 186; bond acknowledged 22 JUL 1796, p. 187.

DIXON, James. Will: ...of the Town of Alexandria; unto my beloved wife Elinor Dixon all the Estate that I now have or may hereafter have both real and personal the before (requisitions being complyed with) to her and the heirs of her body for ever; appoint my beloved wife Elinor Dixon together with my Friends Robert Brocket and Thomas West, the Executors...; dated 7 FEB 1800, /s/ James Dixon, wit. Henry McCue, George Woolls, and Hugh Maxwell, p. 314; proved 3 MAR 1800, pp. 314-315; Eleanor Dixon, Robert Brocket and John Longdon, bound unto justices of the Court of Hustings for the Town of Alexandria now sitting in the sum of $700 to take inventory, dated 3 MAR 1800, pp. 315-316; bond acknowledged, 3 MAR 1800, p. 316.

ELLIS, William. Will: at present in the Town of Alexandria; give to my honoured father Nugent Ellis of the County of Donnegall in the Kingdom of Ireland, all my estate of whatsoever kind or nature; And in case my Father is not at present living or should depart this life before he is informed of this Will then...all my Property shall be equally divided between my Honoured Mother, my Brother John and sisters Martha, and Susanna Ellis; he or said others paying unto Peggy McGouldrick of Killgorden in the County and Kingdom aforesaid the sum of Fifteen Pounds sterling which I do hereby devise and give unto her, and also paying annually unto her son William Ellis Five Pounds sterling per annum until he arrives to the age of Twenty one years...; ordain My Friends William Herbert, Samuel Montgomery Brown and John Reynolds, Executors of this; dated 3 MAY 1785; /s/ William Ellis, wit. John Jolly, Ch. Simms; proved 24 AUG 1786; pp. 1-2; John Ellis, Robert McClanachan, James Hendricks and Thomas Barclay bound unto judges of the Court of Hustings to take inventory, 24 AUG 1786, pp. 2-4; bond acknowledged, 24 AUG 1786, p. 4.

FLOYD, Mary T.C., ward of William Hodgson; William Hodgson and Edmund J. Lee, bound to justices of the Court of Hustings for the Town of Alexandria in the sum of $1,000 for guardianship, dated 5 JAN 1801, pp. 335-336; bond acknowledged, 5 JAN 1801, p. 336.

FLOYD, Thomas. Administrator William Hodgson; William Hodgson and Edmund J. Lee, bound unto Amos Alexander, George Taylor,

Alexandria, Virginia Wills, Administrations and Guardianships

George Slacum and Peter Wise, Jr. in the full and just sum of $1,000 to take inventory, dated 5 JAN 1801, pp. 336-337; bond acknowledged 5 JAN 1801, p. 338.

FRAZER, Stacy. Administrator John Harrell; John Harrel, William Steel and William Davis, bound to justices of the Court of Hustings in Alexandria to take inventory, 23 JAN 1794, pp. 131-132; bond acknowledged 23 JAN 1794, p. 132.

FULFORD, Robert. Will: ...of the Town of Alexandria; to my well beloved Wife Mary Fulford to be intirely at her disposal except so much thereof as may be necessary to pay all my Just Debts; appoint Mary Fulford my Lawfull Executrix; dated 10 NOV 1794, /s/ Robert Fulford, wit. William Halley and Esther Halley, pp. 144-145; proved 18 DEC 1794, p. 145; Mary Fulford, William Halley and William Summers, bound to justices of the Court of Hustings for the Town of Alexandria to take inventory, dated 18 DEC 1794, pp. 145-146; bond acknowledged 18 DEC 1794, p. 147; inventory and appraisement by William Halley, William Paton and Peter Wise, pp. 172-176, returned 24 JUL 1793.

FULTON, Joseph and Robert Fulton, wards of Mary Fulton; Mary Fulton and Wm. Harper; bound unto justices of the Court of Hustings for the Town of Alexandria and their Successors in the sum of £5,000 [sic], dated 8 MAY 1798, pp. 272-273; wit. Wm. Harper and James Grimes; bond acknowledged 8 MAY 1798, p. 273.

FULTON, Robert. Will: ...of the Town of Alexandria; bequeath unto my wife Mary Ann the whole of my real and personal Estate during her widowhood only, and in case of Marriage the said bequeathed Estates unto her is to fall back unto my two children Joseph and Robert Fulton which shall be equally divided amongst them; ordain James Fletcher and Hugh McGahan both of the said Town of Alexandria to be my Executors; dated 28 AUG 1797; /s/ Robert Fulton; wit. Jno. C. Kempff, John Hill and Samuel Keech, pp. 235-236; proved 2 OCT 1797, p. 237; James Fletcher, John Hill and Robert Lauphier, bound unto justices of the Court of Hustings for the Town of Alexandria in the sum of $2,000 to take inventory, dated 2 OCT 1797, pp. 237-239; bond acknowledged, 2 OCT 1797, p. 239; inventory of the goods belonging to the estate of Robert Fulton, deceased, by John Hunter, John Hill and John Hughes, dated 24 OCT 1797, pp. 239-240; inventory of the property belonging to the estate of John Reynolds, deceased, 11 SEP

Alexandria, Virginia Wills, Administrations and Guardianships

1797, by Wm. Harper, Samuel Harper and Samuel Craig, recorded 7 NOV 1797, pp. 241-242; account of James Fletcher, presented 23 JAN 1799, recorded 4 FEB 1799, pp. 282-285.

GRACE, John. Will: In the name of God amen, I, John Grace of the Town of Alexandria, County of Fairfax and State of Virginia...; request that my body may be decently Buried in the Burial Ground of the Roman Catholick Congrigation of the Town of Alexandria; to my Dearly beloved wife Celia Grace the sum of $1,000 to be paid her in cash together with all my plate, and Household Furniture, requesting that at her demise, she may Divide the Plate equally amongst such of my children as may then be alive; the remainder of my property, real and personal (after all my Just and lawfull Debts are paid), I bequeath to my four children, to be equally divided between them, as follows: one fourth part...to my eldest son Samuel Grace, one fourth part to my Second Eldest Son Charles Grace, one Fourth part to my Third Eldest Child Celia Grace, and one Fourth part to my fourth Eldest child Joseph Grace; appoint Guy Atkinson, Matthew Robinson and James Bacon all of the Town of Alexandria and County of Fairfax aforesaid my Sole Executors; appoint my Dearly beloved wife Celia Grace of the Town of Loghrea, County of Galway and Kingdom of Ireland, my sole administratrix, and Matthew Madden of the Town of Loghrea aforesaid, my sole Executor to carry into Effect this my last will and testament in the Kingdom of Ireland, /s/ John Grace, signed, sealed published & declared by the within named John Grace to be his last will & Testament this 27th day of December one thousand seven hundred and ninety nine, in the presence of us, Theophilas Harris, James Kennedy, and John Kincaid, pp. 321-322; schedule of property with an acct. of the sundry debts due to John Grace, p. 323; proved 5 MAY 1800, p. 323; Guy Atkinson, James Bacon, Matthew Robinson, John Foster, Samuel Craig and Philip G. Marsteller, bound unto Amos Alexander, Alexander Smith, William B. Page and Charles Alexander, gent. in the sum of $5,000 to take inventory, dated 5 MAY 1800, pp. 323-324; bond acknowledged 5 JUL 1800, p. 324; order that Philip Marsteller, William Pomery, Joshua Riddle and Samuel McCloud or any three of them...do inventory and appraise all the singular the Estate of John Grace deceased..., May Court 1800, p. 344; inventory by P. Marsteller, William Pomery, Joshua Riddle and Samuel McCloud, presented 3 FEB 1801, pp. 345-348.

Alexandria, Virginia Wills, Administrations and Guardianships

GREENWAY, Joseph, Polly Greenway and Eliza Greenway, wards of William Harper and Rebecca Greenway; William Harper and Rebecca Greenway, James Keith and John Janney, bound to justices of the County Court of Fairfax for guardianship, dated 21 OCT 1796, pp. 202-204; bond acknowledged, 21 OCT 1796, p. 204.

GRETTER, Mary Goulding and Ann Hooff Gretter, wards of Margaret Gretter; Margaret Gretter and John Harper, bound unto justices of the Court of Hustings for the Town of Alexandria in the sum of $1,000 for guardianship, dated 4 NOV 1799, pp. 296-297; bond acknowledged, 4 NOV 1799, p. 297.

HAGERTY, Patrick. Administratrix Margaret Hagerty; Margaret Hagerty, Patrick Burns, Oliver Price and Jacob Hineman, bound to justices of the Court of Hustings to take inventory, 20 AUG 1791, pp. 49-50; bond acknowledged 20 AUG 1791, p. 50; inventory by John Longdon, Morris Worrell and Ralph Longdon, dated 31 AUG 1791, pp. 51-53, recorded 22 SEP 1791, p. 53.

HARDEN, Joseph. Administrator Charles Harden; Charles Harden, Michael Steiber and Thomas Redman, bound to justices of the Court of Hustings in Alexandria to take inventory, dated 18 DEC 1794, pp. 147-148; bond acknowledged, 18 DEC 1794, p. 149.

HARLE, Robert. Administratrix Nancy Harle; Nancy Harle and Jesse Taylor, bound to justices of the Court of Hustings for the Town of Alexandria, dated 23 FEB 1797, pp. 220-221; bond acknowledged, 24 FEB 1797, p. 221.

HARRISON, Barbara. Administrator Philip Marsteller; Philip Marsteller and George Slacum, bound to justices of the Court of Hustings for the Town of Alexandria, dated 20 JAN 1796, pp. 193-194; bond acknowledged, 20 JAN 1797, p. 195; will, I, Barbara Harrison of the Town of Alexandria, ...that after my decease my negro man Aaron shall from thenceforth be emancipated, set free and at Liberty and enjoy all the privileges of a free man, agreeable to my Will herein expressed; /s/ Barbara (her mark) Harrison; wit. 30 SEP 1796 by A. Faw and Alice Lawrason, pp. 197-198; proved 21 OCT 1796, p. 198; order for Alexander Smith and John Boyer, bound to justices of the Court of Hustings to make inventory, incorrectly inscribed for "Samuel" Harrison's estate, dated 21 OCT 1796, pp. 198-201; bond acknowledged 21 OCT 1796, p. 202.

Alexandria, Virginia Wills, Administrations and Guardianships

HARRISON, Samuel. Will: I, Samuel Harrison, of the Town of Alexandria, ...bequeath unto my Brother in Law Thomas Leftridge the Coult which I own cut of the Gray Mare to be delivered to him after my decease. And as to the residue of my Estate of what nature or kind soever the same may be, I give and bequeath unto my loving wife Barbara to be holden by her, her Heirs and Assigns without any Controul whatsoever, she my said wife paying my lawful Debts out of the same. And lastly I do hereby appoint her my said wife Barbara to be the Executrix of this my last will and Testament. In Witness whereof I the said Samuel Harrison have hereunto set my hand and seal this seventh day of Februa. 1796, /s/ Saml. Harrison; wit. George Slacum, P. Marsteller and Philip G. Marsteller, p. 177; proved 19 FEB 1796, pp. 177-178; Barbara Harrison, Philip Marsteller and Philip Marsteller, Jr., bound to justices of the Court of Hustings in the Town of Alexandria to take inventory, dated 19 FEB 1796, pp. 178-179; bond acknowledged 19 FEB 1796, p. 179.

HENRY, John. Inventory returned 2 SEP 1800 by Lanty Crowe, Robert Abercrombie and James Harris, pp. 328-329, recorded 7 OCT 1800, p. 329; Mary Henry, Thomas Swann and George Youngs, bound to justices of the Court of Hustings for the Town of Alexandria now sitting and their successors in the sum of $30 to take inventory, dated 2 SEP 1800, pp. 350-351; bond acknowledged 2 SEP 1800, p. 351.

HOYE, William. Will: ...of the Town of Alexandria; having full confidence in the Prudence and direction of my wife Elizabeth, I do give and devise unto my said wife Elizabeth her Executors Administrators and Assigns the residue of the Term which I have in the house and lott where I now live and all other real and personal estate of which I am seized and possessed, to enable her to educate and bring up my children not in the least doubting her paying every attention to them and rendering them strict Justice. Lastly, I nominate and appoint my said Wife Elizabeth Executrix...; dated 15 DEC 1799, /s/ Wm. Hoye; wit. Jas. Keith, Saml. Hilton, Washer Blunt, and Jacob Leap, pp. 305-306; proved 4 FEB 1800, p. 306; Elizabeth Hoye, George Gilpin and William Harper, bound to justices of the Court of Hustings for the Town of Alexandria now sitting in the sum of $2,000 to take inventory, 4 FEB 1800, pp. 307-308; bond acknowledged 4 FEB 1800, p. 308; inventory by Jno. C. Vowell, Danl. McClean and Jacob Leap, dated 13

Alexandria, Virginia Wills, Administrations and Guardianships

FEB 1800, recorded 3 MAR 1800, pp. 316-318.

HULLS, Robert. Inventory and appraisement by Wm. Summers, James McGuire and Dennis Ramsay, dated 11 APR 1797, recorded 7 JAN 1799, pp. 282-283.

HYSLEY, George. Executrix Mary Hysley; Mary Hysley, Wm. McKnight and John Harper, bound to justices of the Court of Hustings for the Town of Alexandria, dated 21 OCT 1796, pp. 205-206; bond acknowledged, 21 OCT 1796, p. 207.

JONES, John W. Ordered that John Dunlap, Thomas Irvin, Samuel Harper and William Harper or any three of them being first sworn according to Law, do inventory and appraise all and singular the estate of John W. Jones, deceased, that shall be presented to their view..., August Court 1800, pp. 335-336; inventory, dated 4 AUG 1800, by Thomas Irwin, William Harper and Samuel Harper, pp. 332-333, recorded 5 FEB 1801; Elizabeth Jones, the Mother and heir at Law of John W. Jones deceased, by these presents Constitutes and appoints John and Thomas Vowell of Alexandria, administrators of the Estate of said John W. Jones, given in my hand this 2nd day of August 1800, /s/ Elizabeth Jones, wit. Wm. Lyles and Thos. Cooke, p. 348; Thomas Vowell, Jr. and Joseph Harper, bound unto justices of the Court of Hustings for the Town of Alexandria now sitting and their successors in the sum of $3,000 to take inventory, dated 4 AUG 1800, pp. 349-350; bond acknowledged, 4 AUG 1800, p. 350.

KIDD, David. Administrator James Kidd; James Kidd, Thomas Steuart and Duncan Nevin, bound unto justices of the Court of Hustings for the Town of Alexandria to take inventory, dated 3 FEB 1800, pp. 300-103; bond acknowledged 3 FEB 1800, p. 301.

KIRK, Bridget. Administrator Archibald McClean; Archibald McClean and John Neal, bound unto justices of the Court of Hustings for the Town of Alexandria, dated 2 MAY 1797, pp. 224-225; bond acknowledged 2 MAY 1797, p. 225; sales of estate, by order of Mr. A. McLean, admr., 3 JUN 1797, pp. 270-271; inventory and appraisement, by Alexr. Smith, Jas. Keith and Wm. Milner, Jr., pp. 271-272.

KIRK, Harriot, ward of William Jackson; William Jackson, Ellis Price, George Corryell and Adam Lynn, bound unto justices of the Court of Hustings their Heirs and Successors in the sum of $5,000, current money of Virginia, dated 2 JAN 1798, pp. 251-252; bond acknowledged 2 JAN 1798, p. 253.

KIRK, Robert, ward of Archibald McClean; Archibald McClean, William Milner and John V. Thomas, bound unto justices of the Court of Hustings for the Town of Alexandria for guardianship, dated 2 MAY 1797, pp. 226-227; bond acknowledged 2 MAY 1797, p. 227.

LEWIS, Edward. Will: In the name of God, Amen, I, Edward Lewis of the Town of Alexandria, Blacksmith...; to Eliza both my Dearly beloved wife the wole [sic] of my real and persnall [sic] property; I likewise constitute make and ordain the sole Executrix...; friday November the twenty seck [sic] and in the year of our lord one thousand Seven hundred and ninety nine.; /s/ Edward Lewis (his mark), wit. Daniel C. Puppo, Enoch Pelton and Samuel Hilton, pp. 297-298; proved 3 FEB 1800, pp. 298-299; Elizabeth Lewis, George Hill and William Mills, bound unto justices of the Court of Hustings for the Town of Alexandria now sitting in the sum of $700 to take inventory, dated 3 FEB 1800, pp. 299-300; bond acknowledged 3 FEB 1800, p. 300.

LONGDON, Robert. Administrator John Longdon; John Longdon and John V. Thomas, bound unto justices of the Court of Hustings now setting in the sum of $700, dated 5 AUG 1799, pp. 288-289; bond acknowledged 5 AUG 1799, p. 289.

LONGDON, Robert, ward of John Longdon; John Longdon and Richard Weightman, bound to justices of the Court of Hustings for the Town of Alexandria for guardianship, dated 24 APR 1795, pp. 160-161; bond acknowledged 22 APR 1795, p. 161.

LOTHRUP, Seth, Junior. Will: ...all money and property that is due to me and desire that the said money and property may be given to my honored Father Seth Lothrup, Senr.; David Hidie of Charleston, in the State of South Carolina, has a power of atty. to collect wages due me from Capt. Whealen while on Board of the sloop Industry, the sum of Sixty Seven Dollars and five Shillings; Jerusha Spears of the Town of Boston in the State of Massachusets [sic] is Justly indebted to me in the sum of eight hundred Dollars and one suit of cloths and one broatch all left in his possession when I left the Town of Boston; done at the Town of Alexandria in the State of Virginia this 4 day of April 1800, /s/ Seth Lothrup, Junr., wit. Thos. Whittredge, Amos Lefavour and Elizabeth Mason (mark), pp. 318-

319; proved 8 APR 1800, p. 319.

LOWNDS, John. Administrator James Lownds; James Lownds and Aaron Hewes, bound to Amos Alexander, George Taylor, George Slacum and Peter Wise, Junr., in the full and Just sum of $1,000 to take inventory, dated 5 NOV 1800, pp. 362-363; bond acknowledged 6 NOV 1800, p. 363.

LUTZ, Michael. Inventory by Peter Wise, George Darling and John Richter, dated 10 MAR 1796, in obedience to an order of the Court of Hustings, returned 24 SEP 1796, pp. 187-188.

MASON, George. Will: In the Name of God Amen, I George Mason of the Town of Alexandria...I recommend to the earth to be buried in decent christian burial at the discretion of my Executrix nothing doubting but at the General Resurrection I shall Receive the same again by the might power of God...; bequeath to Elizabeth by dearly beloved wife whom I likewise constitute make and ordain the sole Executrix of this my last will and testament, all and singular my lands messuages and tenements together with all my household Goods and moveable Estate...; dated 28 JAN 1795, /s/ George Mason; wit. Geo. Corryell, John Rea, Henry (his mark) McCue, and Alexr. Smith, pp. 180-181; proved 21 MAY 1796; Eliz. Mason and Alexander Smith, bound to justices of the Court of Hustings in the Town of Alexandria to take inventory, dated 21 MAY 1796, pp. 181-182; bond acknowledged, 21 MAY 1796, p. 183; inventory by Alexander McConnell, George Correll and Philip G. Marsteller, dated 21 JUL 1796, returned 24 SEP 1796, pp. 189-190.

McHENRY, Ann. Administrators Jesse Taylor and Patrick Burns; Jesse Taylor, Patrick Burns, Dennis Ramsay and Matthew Robinson, bound unto justices of the Court of Hustings for the Town of Alexandria now sitting and their Successors in the sum of $1,000, dated 3 APR 1798, pp. 266-267; bond acknowledged, 4 APR 1798, p. 267.

McHENRY, James. Administratrix Ann McHenry; Ann McHenry, Jesse Taylor and Patrick Byrnes, bound to justices of the Court of Hustings for the Town of Alexandria to take inventory, dated 20 JAN 1796, pp. 190-191; bond acknowledged 20 JAN 1797, p. 193; inventory by James McClish, James Young and Patr. Byrne, returned 5 FEB 1798, pp. 256-259.

McMASTERS, Charles John, ward of

Alexandria, Virginia Wills, Administrations and Guardianships

Richard Weightman; bond of Richard Weightman and John Longdon, to justices of the Court of Hustings for the Town of Alexandria for guardianship, dated 24 APR 1795, pp. 159-160; acknowledged 22 APR 1795 [sic], p. 160.

McMASTERS, Mary. Administrator Richard Weightman; Richard Weightman and John Longdon bound to justices of the Court of Hustings, dated 24 APR 1795, pp. 157-159; bond acknowledged, 22 APR 1795, p. 159.

McPHERSON, Daniel. Will: ...of the Town of Alexandria, all my debts as well as those which I may owe in my own private capacity, as those which I may owe as one of the partners in the business carried on the name of Daniel and Isaac McPherson may be fully paid as also my funeral expenses; that the business now carried on in the name of Daniel and Isaac McPherson be Immediately closed; all the real property held by Daniel and Isaac McPherson be exposed to sale as soon as my Executors herein after named...and my brother Isaac McPherson shall judge; whereas my Father Daniel McPherson did by his last Will and Testament devise unto my mother during her natural life a part of the land upon which he lived and after her death gave the same to his six younger children to be equally divided among them; unto my wife Martha all my House hold Furniture; unto my nephew Jonas McPherson all my wearing apparel and books; after expenses half of the residue of my Estate unto my wife Martha...and in case my wife should prove to be pregnant at my death I give and devise the other half of the residue of my said Estate to such child...; appoint my wife Martha, Executrix, brother Isaac McPherson, my father in law Edward Beeson, and my friends, William Hartshorne and James Keith, Executors; dated 1 JUN 1790, /s/ Danl. McPherson; wit. James Craik, Math. Ingraham and Thomas Peterkin, pp. 30-34; proved 24 FEB 1791, p. 35; Isaac McPherson, Martha McPherson, Edward Beeson and Josiah Watson bound to justices of the Court of Hustings to take inventory, 24 FEB 1791, pp. 35-36; bond acknowledged 24 FEB 1791, p. 37.

MENDENHALL, William. Inventory dated 20 of 9th Mo. 1796, by Elisha Janney, Philip Wanton and Thomas Fisher, returned 7 OCT 1800, pp. 351-358; accounts, dated 8 JUL 1800 by George Gilpin, pp. 360-361, recorded 7 OCT 1800, p. 362.

MENDENHALL, William, ward of John Janney; John Janney, William Patten and Elisha Janney, bound unto

Alexandria, Virginia Wills, Administrations and Guardianships

justices of the Court of Hustings in the sum of $4,000 for guardianship, dated 23 JAN 1799, p. 282; bond acknowledged [blank] JAN 1799, pp. 281-282.

MERTLAND, John. Administratrix Susanna Mertland; Susanna Mertland and Fredrick Tridle, bound unto justices of the Court of Hustings for the Town of Alexandria now sitting and their Successors in the sum of $200 to take inventory, dated 7 OCT 1800, pp. 358-359; bond acknowledged, 7 OCT 1800, p. 359.

MOODY, Samuel. Administrator John Bogue; John Bogue, James McHenry and John Lumsdon, bound to justices of the Court of Hustings in the Town of Alexandria to take inventory, dated 25 SEP 1795, p. 163; bond acknowledged, 25 SEP 1795, p. 164.

MOODY, Samuel. Will: **In the Name of God, Amen.** Be it known unto all then that I Samuel Moody this thirty first day of August one thousand seven hundred and ninety five, finding myself indisposed but in sound judgment, and clear recollection, do make this my last will and testament; after my just debts and funeral expenses are paid, the remainder to be duly collected and remitted to my Father and Mother or nearest Relative in England, for this purpose. I do hereby appoint John Bogue, Joiner, in the Town of Alexandria, Virginia, fully empowering him to collect all just Debts as aforesaid, and to pay all lawfull Debts. /s/ Saml. Moody; wit. William Moxley, Benjamin Davidson, and John Lumsdon, pp. 170-171. Herewith I subjoin an Inventory of my Goods &c., one Box of wearing apparel at Buckley's, one Chest of Tools at Do. and one fowling piece, one new Chest wt. some Tools at Mr. Ross's, sundry cloaths at Mr. Ross's, two Great Coats (not in my Box) at Mr. Buckley's, a silver watch, at William Moxley's; p. 171; proved 25 SEP 1795, p. 171; list of sales, incorrectly inscribed "Thomas" Moody, dated 5 JAN 1796, returned 22 JUL 1796, p. 185.

MOORE, George. Administrator William Summers; William Summers and John Longdon, bound to justices of the Court of Hustings to take inventory, 22 SEP 1791, pp. 53-55; bond acknowledged 22 SEP 1791, p. 55.

MULLEN, Patrick. Inventory by John Janney, Philip Wanton and Jno. Watts, dated 10 JAN 1797, recorded 20 JAN 1797, pp. 196-197; administrator Thomas Mullen; Thomas Mullen and Bryan Hampson, bound to justices of the Court of Hustings for the town of Alexandria, dated 23 DEC 1796, pp. 209-212; bond acknowledged, 23 DEC 1796, p. 212.

MUMFORD, John. Administrator John A. Steuart; John A. Steuart, Jesse Taylor and Peter Wise, bound unto justices of the Court of Hustings for the Town of Alexandria now setting and their Successors in the sum of $5,000, dated 4 MAR 1799, pp. 286-287; bond acknowledged, 4 MAR 1799, p. 287.

NOUVOULET, Jeane Marie. Administrator Paul Arnold Sherue; Paul Arnold Sherue, James Neblon and John Pettit, bound to justices of the Court of Hustings in Alexandria, 19 DEC 1793, pp. 128-129; bond acknowledged 18 DEC 1793, p. 129.

OWENS, William. Administrator William Myers; William Myers and Richard Lewis, bound unto justices of the Court of Hustings for the Town of Alexandria now sitting and their Successors in the sum of $200 to take inventory, dated 3 MAR 1800, pp. 308-309; bond acknowledged 3 MAR 1800, p. 309; inventory by Danl. Bishop, Bernard Bryan and Theos. Harris, recorded 3 JUN 1800, p. 328.

PENDLE, Thomas. Administrator Lewis Weston; Lewis Weston and Philip Marsteller, bound unto justices of the Court of Hustings to take inventory, dated 23 JAN 1794, pp. 134-136; bond acknowledged 23 JAN 1794, p. 136.

PORTER, Thomas. Administratrix Sarah Porter; Sarah Porter, John Ramsay, Jesse Taylor and Dennis Ramsay, bound unto justices of the Court of Hustings for the Town of Alexandria now sitting and their Successors in the sum of $6,000 to take inventory, 9 JUL 1800, pp. 325-326; bond acknowledged, p. 326.

PRATT, Margaret. Administrator William Summers; William Summers and Joh[n] Longdon bound to justices of the Court of Hustings to take inventory, 23 JUN 1791, pp. 41-42; bond acknowledged 23 JUN 1791, p. 43.

RAMSAY, William. Will: **In the Name of God Amen**, I William Ramsay of the County of Fairfax and Commonwealth of Virginia...; give and bequeath to my son William Ramsay, alias William Tucker, born of Sarah, alias Sally Tucker of Boston in the State of Massachusetts Bay, and the lawful begotten heirs of his Body, all the real and personal Estate I may die possessed forever. But he shall yearly, or as near it as possible, allow his Mother during her life a maintenance, that shall in the opinion of two or three just and properly qualified persons, be deemed suitable to the possessions I may leave him. If I should hereafter marry, and have a child, he is then only to have two shares of my Estate real and personal to him and his Heirs as aforesaid, and the child afterwards so born to have the remainder of my Estate both real and personal in fee simple forever, if more than one child be afterwards born, I give and devise to them and their heirs forever the said the said [sic] remainder of my Estate to be equally devided between them, if my son William aforesaid should die under the age of twenty one years, not leaving issue of his Body lawfully begotten and I should leave no other Child, I give and devise unto his Mother Sarah Tucker aforesaid during her life the sum of seventy pounds per Annum, to be paid out of the Rents and profits of my Estate, and devise the remainder of my Estate real and personal to my Brother and sisters and their Heirs equally to be divided between them. In Witness whereof I have this twenty first day of July in the year of our Lord one thousand seven hundred and Eighty seven, affixed my hand and seal. /s/ William Ramsay. Witnesses D. Arell, Wm. Hunter, Moses Tandy, and Geo. Richards. Proved 21 SEP 1795, pp. 169-170.

REDMAN, Thomas. Administrator Thomas Redman; Thomas Redman and Michael Stieber bound to gentlemen [justices] of the Court of Hustings, 19 OCT 1792, pp. 83-84; bond acknowledged, 19 OCT 1792, p. 84

REDMAN, Thomas. Will: In the name of God Amen, I, Thomas Redman being weak in health but still in Sound memory of mind blessed be the almighty do hereby make my last Will and Testament, first I command my Soul to the Almighty who has given it to me & as for my Estate which God has bestowed to me I leave all my real & personal Estate unto my beloved wife & heir Sarah Redman & heir in paying off my Just & lawfull debts, In Witness whereof I have hereunto set my hand & affixed my Seal this 20th day of January 1800, /s/ Ths. (his mark) Redmond, wit. D. Kempff, Henry McCue, Garret Doyle and Robert Evans, p. 319; proved 8 APR 1800, p. 320; Sarah Redman, Henry McCue and Robert Evans, bound unto justices of the Court of Hustings for the Town of Alexandria now sitting and their Successors in the sum of $1,000 to take inventory, dated 8 APR 1800, pp. 320-321; bond acknowledged 8 APR 1800, p. 321; order for inventory, April Court 1800, p. 326; inventory by John Horner, Saml.

Craig and John Foster, p. 327, recorded 3 JUN 1800, p. 328.

REYNOLDS, John. Administratrix Sarah Reynolds; Sarah Reynolds and Benjamin Shreeve, bound unto justices of the Court of Hustings for the Town of Alexandria, dated 7 AUG 1797, pp. 231-233; bond acknowledged, 7 AUG 1797, p. 233.

RICK, William. Administratrix Christiana Rick; Christiana Rick, Philip Marsteller and William Hickman, bound to justices of the Court of Hustings in Alexandria to take inventory, 20 DEC 1792, pp. 117-118; bond acknowledged, 20 DEC 1792, p. 119; appraisement (chiefly copper smith tools and supplies) by John Yost, John Longdon and Andrew Reintzel, pp. 119-123, dated 2 JAN 1793, recorded 24 JAN 1793, p. 124; account of Christiana Rick, presented 23 JAN 1794, pp. 137-140.

ROBINSON, Sarah. Administrator William Herbert; William Herbert and George Deneale bound to justices of the Court of Hustings to take inventory, 24 APR 1788, pp. 9-11; bond acknowledged 24 FEB 1788, p. 11.

SAUNDERS, John. Will: ...unto my wife Mary the use of all my Estate real and personal until my Daughter Sarah arrives to the age of twenty one years for the Purpose of bringing up and Educating my children in a manner suitable...; rest of my said Estate...unto my said wife until my Son Peter shall arrive to the age of Twenty one years, fifth part of my said Estate; unto my said wife Mary until my Son David arrives to the age of twenty one years...fifth part of my said Estate; I have some pieces of Ground in the Town of Alexandria unoccupied and unimproved, I do hereby authorize and empower by Executors...grant them...proper rents; unto my said wife during her natural Life and after her death I give and Devise the whole of my Estate unto the children of my several sisters who may be born or living at that time...; appoint my wife Mary, Executrix and my friends William Hartshorne, Benjamin Shreeve and John Butcher, Executors; dated 13 5th Mo. 1790, /s/ John Saunders; wit. Jas. Keith, John Dowdall and Robert Lyle, pp. 24-28; proved 24 AUG 1790, p. 28; Mary Saunders, William Hartshorne and George Gilpin, bound to justices of the Court of Hustings to take inventory, 24 AUG 1790, pp. 29-30; bond acknowledged 24 AUG 1790, p. 30; inventory by George Gilpin, William Patton and Jonah Thompson, dated 15 JAN 1791, returned 21 JUL 1791, pp. 43-48.

Alexandria, Virginia Wills, Administrations and Guardianships

SAUNDERS, Sarah, Peter Saunders and David Saunders, wards of Philip Wanton; Philip Wanton, Samuel Craig, Alexander Smith and John T. Ricketts, bound to justices of the Court of Hustings in the sum of $10,000 for guardianship, dated 5 SEP 1797, pp. 233-234; bond acknowledged, 4 SEP 1797, pp. 234-235.

SHAW, William. Administrator William Summers; William Summers and Job Green, bound to justices of the Court of Hustings for the Town of Alexandria, dated 24 APR 1795, pp. 149-150, and the same so made do exhibit or cause to be Exhibited into the County Court of Fairfax...; bond acknowledged, 24 APR 1795, p. 151.

SHROPSHIRE, William. Will: I, William Shropshire, of the Town of Alexandria in the state of Virginia, do make Ordain this to be my Last will and Testament in manner and form following to wit.; Whereas my father William Shropshire did by his will devise his Estate to his three sons James, John and myself, to be divided among us at a certain period but my said father being in debt at the time of his death it has been concluded to let the Estate remain undivided until those debts were discharged among other articles of which that Estate consists there are some Slaves one or more of which may probably [sic] be allotted unto me. Now it is my desire in case of the allotment of any of those slaves unto me in the division of the said Estate and I do hereby order and direct that such slave or slaves in case of being a female or females and at this time under the age of Twenty one years be Emancipated at the age of Twenty five years, and if the slave or slaves so allotted prove to be males and at this time under the age of Twenty one years then that such slave or slaves be Emancipated at the age of Twenty Eight years...; all my estate real and personal as well what I am at this time seized and possessed of in my own right as Whatever part of my father estate may be allotted me...unto my wife Elizabeth untill my daughter Eliza Windsor Shropshire shall arive [sic] to the age of Twenty one years or Marry which ever Event shall first take place; appoint My friends Mordecai Miller and Henry Stanton Earle, Executors...; 9 JUN 1800, /s/ Wm. Shropshire, wit. James Keith, L. Mansfield and Anna (her mark) Sloan, pp. 338-341; proved 6 JAN 1801, pp. 341-342; Henry S. Earle, Mordecai Miller and George Slacum, bound unto Amos Alexander, George Slacum, Charles Alexander, Junr. and Peter Wise, Junr., justices of the Court of Hustings holden for Town

Alexandria, Virginia Wills, Administrations and Guardianships

of Alexandria in the just and full sum of $2,000 to take inventory, dated 6 MAY 1801, pp. 342-344; bond acknowledged 6 JAN 1801, p. 344.

SPANGERBURGH, Frederick. Administrator John Stewart; John Stewart, William McKnight and John Longdon bound to justices of the County Court of Fairfax to take inventory, 21 APR 1791, pp. 37-39; bond acknowledged 21 APR 1791, p. 39.

STONE, Robert. Administrator Thomas Mezarvey; Thomas Mezarvey, Thomas Irwin and Francis Peyton, bound unto justices of the Court of Hustings in the Town of Alexandria, dated 23 DEC 1796, pp. 216-219; bond acknowledged, 23 DEC 1796, p. 219; inventory by Thomas Irwin, John Boyer and Thomas Crandel, dated 26 JAN 1797, pp. 230-231.

STUART, James Montgomery, ward of Robert Mease; Robert Mease, Robert Allison and Thomas Porter, bound unto justices of the Court of Hustings for the Town of Alexandria in the sum of $2,000, dated 7 MAY 1798, pp. 287-288; wit. John Morris and John Dayly, Junr.; recorded 7 MAY 1798, p. 288.

SULLIVAN, Timothy. Administratrix Elizabeth Sullivan; Elizabeth Sullivan, John Longdon and Andrew Telefro, bound unto justices of the Court of Hustings for the Town of Alexandria now sitting and their Successors in the sum of $1,500, dated 2 JAN 1798, pp. 253-254; bond acknowledged 2 JAN 1798, p. 254; inventory by Jno. V. Thomas, John Davis, Junr. and Joseph Ingle, dated 3 JAN 1798, pp. 255-256.

SUMMERS, William. Will: **In the Name of God Amen.** I, William Summers, of the Town of Alexandria, of sound and disposed mind, but labouring under some bodily Infirmities to remove which, a voyage to the West Indies is advised, and if Providence should not spare me to see the land of my Nativity again, do make the following disposition of my Estate Real and personal; dispose of an half acre Lott Situate at the corner of Pitt and Princess Streets if other resources should be insufficient; to my three Little Children Elenor, Jane and Harvey Summers all the Vacant Ground on Queen East of the House (and a four foot Alley), I now live in to be equally divided between them when the Eldest comes to the Age of Eighteen or marrys as the case may be...; to my affectionate wife Isabel Summers during her natural life all the residue of my Estate both real and personal, charging the Same with the Education, Maintenance and

Alexandria, Virginia Wills, Administrations and Guardianships

proper can of the three Children above mentioned and after her decease my Will is that all my Estate be then equally divided among my Children and their legal Representatives; to Sytha Cooper (an Orphan girl now in our family) a feather Bed and furniture when she arrives at the Age of Eighteen years which my Wife is to give her cut of my personal Estate; to my son Harvey Summers one share in the Alexandria Library Company, the yearly subscription to said company I desire my Executors to pay out of the profits of my Estate; to my Brother George Summers all my law books and to my Nephew Lewis Summers Six Vollums [sic] of Popes Works; lastly, I appoint my wife Isabel Summers and my Brother George Summers, Executrix and Executor...; dated 26 APR 1796, /s/ Wm. Summers; wit. S. Summers, John Sloan, James Milan and Thos. Summers, pp. 242-244; codicil; invest my Executrix and Executor with full power to convey to Samuel Adams that Lott of Land in the Town of Alexandria which I lately purchest [sic] of the Executors of William Ramsay, deceast [sic]...; that my Executrix and Executor act as Testamentary Guardians to my children and provide there [sic] Maintenance Education &c.; that Negro Jim be free on the 25th day of December 1801, and that Nan be free in ten years from this date, and that Nans child Elijah be free at the Expiration of Twenty four years from this date and be taught to Read and Right, and if Nan should have any more Children during her Servitude my will and desire is that the male be free at Twenty five years of age, and the feemales [sic] at twenty two, and to receive a like Education; I hereby revoke the Lagacy [sic] as mentioned in my will given to Sytha Cooper a Bed and furniture and leave the same to the discretion of my Executrix; dated 7 OCT 1797, pp. 245-247; proved 7 NOV 1797, p. 247; George Summers, John Longdon and George Deneale, bound unto justices of the Court of Hustings for the Town of Alexandria in the sum of $8,000 to take inventory, dated 7 NOV 1797, pp. 247-249; bond acknowledged, 7 NOV 1797, p. 249; Isabell Summers, Henry S. Earle and Bernard Bryan, bound unto justices of the Court of Hustings for the Town of Alexandria, dated 5 OCT 1797, pp. 249-251; bond acknowledged 5 DEC 1797, p. 251; bond for inventory certified 10 JAN 1798, p. 279; inventory (containing negroes Jim, Nan and Elijah) by John Longdon, Aaron Hewes and Wm. Paton, recorded 5 NOV 1798, pp. 279-282.

TAYLOR, Jesse. Administrator Jesse

Taylor; Jesse Taylor and Dennis Ramsay bound to justices of the Court of Hustings in Alexandria, 19 DEC 1793, pp. 126-127; bond acknowledged 18 DEC 1793, p. 127.

TEARNE, Simon. Administrator John McClanachan; John McClanachan and Roger West bound to justices of the Court of Hustings to take inventory, 25 SEP 1789, pp. 12-13; bond acknowledged 25 SEP 1789, p. 14; inventory, pp. 14-16, returned by Nicholas Hannah, George Hill and Adam Butt, filed 22 APR 1790.

TUCKER, William (alias Ramsay), ward of Dennis Ramsay; Dennis Ramsay and Andrew Wales, bound to justices of the Court of Hustings for the Town of Alexandria for guardianship, dated 25 SEP 1795, p. 162; bond acknowledged, 25 SEP 1795, p. 162.

WALES, Andrew. Will: ...of the Town of Alexandria; all my Estate real and personal unto my friends Thomas Vowell Junr. and John Boyer and the Survivor of them and the heirs of such Survivor in Trust to and for the uses and purposes hereinafter mentioned; to my niece Margaret Low or apply the same in such manner as she shall direct during the life of her husband Thomas Low; David Low, James Low, William Low, Joannah Low and Thomas Low, the children of the said Margaret Low by the said Thomas Low do severally attain the age of twenty one years, rent out my said houses and receive the rents and apply the same in such manner as to them shall appear most conclusive to the Interest of the said children; appoint Thomas Vowell, Junior, and John Boyer, Executors...; [blank] 1799, /s/ Andw. Wales; wit. Thomas Crandle, Jas. Keith and John C. Vowell, pp. 302-303; proved 4 FEB 1800, pp. 303-304; Thomas Vowell, Junr., John Boyer and John C. Vowell, bound unto justices of the Court of Hustings for the Town of Alexandria now sitting in the sum of $3,000 to take inventory, dated 4 FEB 1800, pp. 304-305; bond acknowledged, 4 FEB 1800, p. 305; order to Thomas Crandall, Samuel Harper, James Lawrason and John Dunlap or any three of them to inventory estate, February Court 1800, pp. 333-334; inventory by Thomas Crandall, Samuel Harper and John Dunlap, returned 5 JAN 1800, pp. 334-334 [two pages with same number at which point book pagination is off].

WARDEN, William. Administratrix Ann Warden, Ann Warden, Joseph Fullmore and Dedrick Shakle, bound to justices of the Court of Hustings to take inventory, 23 JUN 1792, pp. 81-82; bond acknowledged, 23 JUN

Alexandria, Virginia Wills, Administrations and Guardianships

1792, p. 82.

WESTON, Lewis. Will: **In the Name of God Amen.** I, Lewis Weston, shipwright of Alexandria, Fairfax County and State of Virginia, being weak of body, but of sound and disposing mind, Knowing the certainty of death and the uncertainty of the time thereof do make publish and declare this to be my last Will and Testament, hereby revoking all others.

Imprimis, I give and bequeath my soul to almighty God that gave it and my body to the earth to be enterred at the discretion of my Executors, hereafter named and my Worldly substance wherewith god hath blessed me, I give as follows. I give and bequeath the framed House and [page 152] **Lott** with the use of the Alley to the South, situate on Water Street to my Loving wife Mary Weston, during her natural life and after her decease to be sold by my Executors or the Survivor of them, and the money arising from the sale to be equally divided among my Children or the Surviving of them and the Legal descendants of such as shall be dead before their mother.

Item, that the brick House, adjoining the Framed House and situate on Water Street, be sold by my Executors, herein after named, at the Expiration of five years or sooner if an adequate price can be had for the same and the money arising from the sale to be applied to the payment of all my Just debts and the surplus to be applyed in the most advantageous manner towards supporting and Educating my children while in a state of minority. I also desire that my daughter Sarah and my two sons Lewis and John, may be Educated in a manner equal to the finances of my Estate and I further direct and desire, that my three Daughters, Polly, Elizabeth and Sally, should have from the General Stock, (besides an equal part as before bequeathed) a Genteel suit of Cloaths to be married in as they may respectively engage in a matrimonial State.

Item, I give and bequeath to my children all that [page 153] **Lott** or half acre of ground situate at the corner of St. Asaph and Gibbons Street, containing half an acre to be Equally divided among them, and my desire is that as they Respectively come of age or wish to Improve that Commissioners may be Appointed to plott each their respective proportions, who is to account for and pay toward the ground rents, a proportionable part thereof, equal to the proportion they hold of the Lott, and my further desire is that if my Executors should have any surplus money belonging to my Estate, that they pay the proportion of ground rent, that may be charged to any of

Alexandria, Virginia Wills, Administrations and Guardianships

my Children during their minority or Nonage, the Legacies given to my Children, is hereby made to them their Heirs and Assigns forever.

Item, I desire that my Executors herein after named take the most Effectual and early method of prosecuting to decision, the dispute now pending in the district Court wherein I am plaintiff and Dennis Ramsay, surviving obligor of Daniel Roberdeau are defendants, and that the money recovered (if any) be charged with the several Appropriations heretofore made, and also that they commence suit, against John Mullichan of George Town, State of Maryland, on his bond, apply the money as before to aid a General fund.

Item, I give and bequeath to my Loving wife [page 154] **Mary Weston** a negro woman named Frances during the life of my said wife and at her decease my Will is that the said Negro Frances should be free, and should she at any time by Informaties be rendered Incapable of supporting herself my desire is that she may have a reasonable support from my Estate, I also give my said wife all my Household furniture, she furnishing each of my daughters with a feather bed and furniture as they may respectively engage in matrimony.

And Lastly, I appoint my Loving wife Mary Weston Executrix and my friends Samuel Arell and William Summers, Executors of this my last Will and Testament. **Witness** my hand this 26th day of March 1795.

Lewis Weston [seal]

Signed, Sealed, Published and declared to be the Last Will & Testament of Lewis Weston in the presence of us who signed the same at his request and in the presence of each other,
Philip G. Marsteller
Thos. Rogerson
James Keith, Jr.
H.R. H<u>oo</u>e, Sr.

Pages 151-154; proved 22 APR 1795, p. 154; Mary Weston, Samuel Arell, William Summers, Philip G. Marsteller and Absalom Wroe, bound to justices of the Court of Hustings for the Town of Alexandria to take inventory, dated 24 APR 1795, pp. 155-156; bond acknowledged, 22 APR 1795 [sic], p. 157.

His Letters of Administration Approbation of such Testament being first had and made in the said Court, Then this obligation to be void else to remain in full force and virtue

Sealed & Delivered   Wm Summers (Seal)
In presence of   Job Green (Seal)
The Court

At a Court of Hustings held for the Town of Alexandria 24th April 1795. William Summers and Job Greene acknowledged this Bond to be their act and Deed, which is ordered to be recorded.

           Test D Wagoner C.C.

In the Name of God Amen

I Lewis Weston Shipwright of Alexandria, Fairfax County and State of Virginia, being weak of body, but of sound and disposing mind, Knowing the certainty of death and the uncertainty of the time thereof do make publish and declare this to be my last Will and Testament, hereby revoking all others

Imprimis, I give and bequeath my soul to almighty God that gave it, and my body to the earth to be interred at the descretion of my Executors hereafter named and my Worldly substance wherewith god hath blessed me I give as follows, I give and bequeath the promised House and

Lott, with the use of the Alley to the South, situate on Water Street to my Loving wife Mary Weston, during her natural life and after her decease to be sold by my Executors or the Survivor of them, and the money arising from the sale to be equally divided among my Children or the Surviving of them and the Legal descendants of such as shall be dead before their mother.

Item, my desire is that the brick House, adjoining the Framed House and situate on Water Street, be sold by my Executors herein after named, at the Expiration of five years or sooner if an adequate price can be had for the same and the money arising from the sale to be applied to the payments of all my Just debts and the surplus to be Applyed in the most advantageous manner towards supporting and Educating my Children, while in a state of minority, I also desire that my daughter Sarah and my two sons Lewis and John, may be Educated in a manner equal to the finances of my Estate and I further direct and desire, that my three Daughters, Polly, Elizabeth and Sally, should have from the General Stock, (besides an Equal part as before bequeathed) a Genteel suit of Cloaths to be married in as they may respectively engage in a matrimonial state.

Item I give and bequeath to my Children all that

Lott or half acre of ground situate at the corner of St Asaph and Gibbins Street, containing half an Acre to be Equally divided among them, and my desire is that as they Respectively come to the age or wish to Improve that Commissioners may be Appointed to allott, each their respective proportions, who is to account for and pay toward the ground rent, a proportionable part thereof, equal to the proportion they hold of the Lott, and my farther desire is that if my Executors should have any surplus money belonging to my Estate, that they pay the proportion of ground rent, that may be charged to any of my Children during their minority or Nonage, the Legacies given to my Children, is hereby made to them their Heirs and Assigns forever —

Item I desire that my Executors, herein after named take the most Effectual and early method of prosecuting to decision, the dispute now pending in the district Court wherein I am plaintiff and Dennis Ramsay, surviving Obliger of Daniel Roberdeau are defendants and that the money recovered (if any) be charged with the several Appropriations heretofore made, and also that they commence suit, against Mr. Mullichan of George Town, State of Maryland, on his bond, Apply the money as before to aid a General fund — —

Item, I give and bequeath to my Loving wife —

Mary Weston a negro woman named Frances during the life of my said wife; and at her decease my Will is that the said Negro Frances should be free; and should she at any time by Infirmaties be rendered Incapable of supporting herself my desire is that she may have a reasonable support from my Estate, I also give my said wife all my Household furniture, she furnishing each of my daughters with a feather bed and furniture as they may respectively engage in matrimony —

And Lastly I appoint my Loving wife Mary Weston Executrix and my friends Samuel Arell and William Simmons, Executors of this my last Will and Testament. Witness my hand this 26th day of March 1795.
Signed, Sealed, Published and
declared to be the Last Will & Testament   Lewis Weston (Seal)
of Lewis Weston, in the presence of us who
signed the same at his request and
in the presence of each other
Philip S. Marsteller, Thos Rogerson
James Keith Jr, Wm Hodges

At a Court of Hustings held for the Town of Alexandria 28th April 1795. This Last Will and Testament of Lewis Weston deceased was presented in Court by Mary Weston, Samuel Arell & William

Summers, Executrix and Executors therein named, who made oath thereto, and the same being proved by the oath of Philip G. Marsteller, Thomas Rogerson, and James Keith, is admitted to record, and the said Executors having performed what the Laws require a Certificate is granted them for obtaining a probate thereof in due form.

E.P.   Test. D. Wagoner D. Clk.

Know all Men by these presents that we Mary Weston, Samuel Arell, William Summers, Philip G. Marsteller and Absalom Wice, are held & firmly bound to John Dundas, Josiah Thompson, Francis Peyton, and William Hichman, Gentlemen Justices of the Court of Hustings for the Town of Alexandria now sitting in the sum of Five thousand Dollars, to the payment whereof well and truly to be made to the said Justices and their successors, we bind ourselves, and each of us our and each of our Heirs Executors and Administrators, jointly and severally firmly by these presents, sealed with our seals and dated this 24th day of April in the year of our Lord, one thousand seven hundred and Ninety five. The Condition of the above obligation is such that, if the above bound, Mary, Samuel and William, Executrix and Executors of the Last Will and Testament of Lewis Weston deceased do make or cause to be made a true and perfect

INDEX

"Lomax's addition" 3
"Preston" iv
"Ravensworth" 4
"Rich Hill" 3
"Threlkeld's addition" 4

0
   Aaron 32
   Elijah 44
   Frances 47
   Jim 44
   Nan 44

ABERCROMBIE
   Robert 33
ADAMS
   Samuel 44
ALEXANDER
   Amos 26-29, 31, 36, 42
   Charles . . iv, 2-4, 10, 26, 31, 42
   Frances B. iv
Alexandria Library Company . . . 44
ALLISON
   Francis 1
   Mary 1
   Robert 43
   William 1
ANDERSON
   Elizabeth 1
   Margaret 1
   Ninian 1
   Robert 1
ARELL
   D. 40
   Samuel 47

ATKINS
   Michael 1
ATKINSON
   Guy 31

BACON
   James 26, 31
BADEN
   John B. 2
   Peggy 2
BARBER
   John 2
   Sarah 2
BARCLAY
   Thomas 29
BEESON
   Edward 37
BISHOP
   Daniel 39
BLUNT
   Washer 1, 33
BOA
   Cavan 2
   Margaret 2
BOGUE
   John 38
BOYER
   John 25, 26, 32, 43, 45
BRILLATT
   Thomas 2
BROCKET
   Robert 1, 29
BROCKETT
   Robert 26

BROWN
   Catharine 4, 11
   Catherine 4-6
   Child 3
   Daniel 2
   Frances iv
   Gustavus 3-6
   Gustavus R. 3, 6, 10
   Helen 4-6
   Richard 3-5
   Samuel M. 29
   Sarah 4-6
   William 2, 3, 6, 10
   Windsor 25
BRYAN
   Bernard 1, 39, 44
BUCKLEY
   Mr. 38
BURNETT
   Charles 25
   George 25
   Sarah 25
BURNS
   Patrick 2, 32, 36
BUSHBY
   William 1
BUTCHER
   John 41
BUTT
   Adam 25, 45
   Jacob 25
BUTTS
   Adam 26
   Jacob 26
BYRNE
   Patrick 36
BYRNES
   Patrick 36

CAMPBELL
   Gustavus B. 9, 10
   John 5
CARSON
   Jemima 1
CAVERLY
   James 26
CHAPMAN
   William 26
CHEW
   Roger 26
COCK
   William 26
COLLIER
   Thomas 1
COMPTON
   Wilson 7
CONWAY
   Richard 6
COOKE
   Thomas 34
COOPER
   Sytha 44
COPPER
   Elizabeth 26
   Nancy 26
   Samuel 26
   Sarah 26
CORRELL
   George 36
CORRYELL
   George 34, 36
CORYELL
   George 25
CRAIG
   Samuel 31, 40, 42
CRAIK
   James 26, 37
CRANDALL
   Thomas 45

CRANDEL
  Thomas 43
CRANDLE
  Thomas 45
CRAWLEY
  David 5
CROUCHER
  Thomas 26
CROWE
  Lanty 33
CURTAIN
  Catharine 27
  Daniel 26-28
  Elenor 27
  Elizabeth 27
  Susanna 27
  William 27
CURTZ
  Nicholas 28

DARLING
  George 36
DAVENPORT
  James 25
DAVIS
  Hannah A. 28
  John 43
  Joseph 28
  Mary 28
  Samuel 28
  Sarah 28
  William 30
DAVISON
  Benjamin 38
DAYLY
  John 43
DEEBLE
  William 28
DENEALE
  George 26, 41, 44

DEWER
  George 28
DICK
  Archibald 28
  Elisha C. 28
  Julia 28
DIXON
  Eleanor 29
  Elinor 29
  James 29
DOWDALL
  John 41
DOYLE
  Garret 40
DUFFY
  John 28
DUNLAP
  John 34, 45
DUVALL
  William 1, 26
DYSON
  Joseph 2

EARLE
  Henry S. 42, 44
EBERT
  Adam 28
ELLIS
  John 29
  Martha 29
  Nugent 29
  Susanna 29
  William 29
EVANS
  Robert 40

FAW
  A. 32
  Abraham 26

FERNEAU
  Philip 5
FISHER
  Thomas 37
FITZGERALD
  John 11
FLETCHER
  James 30, 31
FLOYD
  Mary T.C. 29
  Thomas 29
FOLEY
  Dennis 2, 26
FOSTER
  John 26, 31, 40
FRAZER
  Stacy 30
FULFORD
  Mary 30
  Robert 30
FULLMORE
  Joseph 45
FULTON
  Fulton 30
  Joseph 30
  Mary 30
  Mary A. 30
  Robert 30

GIBSON
  Isaac 28
GILPIN
  George 6, 26, 33, 37, 41
GRACE
  Celia 31
  Charles 31
  John 31
  Joseph 31
  Samuel 31

GREEN
  Job 42
GREENWAY
  Eliza 32
  Joseph 32
  Polly 32
  Rebecca 32
GRETTER
  Ann H. 32
  Margaret 32
  Mary G. 32
  Michael 25
GRIMES
  James 30

HADDEUR
  Jane 1
HAGERTY
  Margaret 32
  Patrick 32
HALLEY
  Esther 30
  William 30
HAMPSON
  Bryan 38
HANNAH
  Nicholas 45
HARDEN
  Charles 32
  Joseph 32
HARLE
  Nancy 32
  Robert 32
HARPER
  Charles 28
  John 32, 34
  Joseph 34
  Samuel 31, 34, 45
  William 2, 28, 31-34

HARRELL
  John 30
HARRIS
  James 33
  Theophilas 31
  Theos. 39
HARRISON
  Barbara 32, 33
  Mr. 3
  Samuel 32, 33
HARTSHORNE
  William 27, 28, 37, 41
HEMSLEY
  Mr. 3
HENDRICKS
  James 29
HENRY
  John 33
  Mary 33
HERBERT
  William 6, 29, 41
HEWES
  Aaron 28, 36, 44
  Abram 28
HICKMAN
  William 41
HIDIE
  David 35
HILL
  George 35, 45
  John 30
HILTON
  Samuel 33, 35
HINEMAN
  Jacob 32
HODGSON
  William 29
HOOE
  H.R. 47
  Mr. 3
HORNER
  John 40
HOYE
  Elizabeth 33
  William 33
HUGHES
  John 30
HULLS
  Robert 34
HUNTER
  John 30
  William 4, 40
HYSLEY
  George 34
  Mary 34

INGLE
  Joseph 43
INGRAHAM
  Math. 37
IRVIN
  Thomas 34
IRWIN
  Thomas 34, 43

JACKSON
  William 34
JANNEY
  Elisha 37
  John 32, 37, 38
JOLLY
  John 29
JONES
  Charles 28
  Elizabeth 34
  John W. 34

KEECH
  Samuel 30

KEITH
    Isaac S. 1
    James   11, 28, 32-34, 37, 41, 42,
                               45, 47
KEMPFF
    D. 40
    John C. 26, 30
KENNEDY
    James 11, 26, 31
KIDD
    David 34
    James 34
KINCAID
    John 31
KIRK
    Bridget 34
    Harriot 34
    Robert 35
KYGER
    Mr.? 27

LAFAVOUR
    Amos 35
LAKE
    Casina 26
LAUPHIER
    Robert 30
LAWRASON
    Alice 32
    James 2, 45
LEAP
    Jacob 33
LEAR
    Tobias 1
LEE
    Edmund J. 29
LEFTRIDGE
    Thomas 33
LEWIS
    Edward 35

    Eliza 35
    Elizabeth 35
    Richard 28, 39
LIMRICK
    John 2
LONGDON
    John . 26, 29, 32, 35, 37-39, 41, 4
                              3, 44
    Ralph 32
    Robert 35
LOTHRUP
    Seth 35
LOW
    David 45
    James 45
    Joannah 45
    Margaret 45
    Thomas 45
    William 45
LOWNDS
    James 36
    John 36
LUMSDON
    John 1, 38
LUTZ
    Michael 36
LYLE
    Robert 26, 41
LYLES
    William 34
LYNN
    Adam 34

MADDEN
    Matthew 31
MAINNING
    Robert 10
MANSFIELD
    L. 42

MARSTELLER
  Philip 1, 26, 31-33, 39, 41
  Philip G. 31, 33, 36, 47
MASON
  Elizabeth 35, 36
  George 36
MAXWELL
  Hugh 29
McCASLAND
  Hannah 1
McCLANACHAN
  John 45
  Robert 29
McCLEAN
  Archibald 34, 35
  Daniel 33
McCLISH
  Archibald 1, 28
  James 1, 36
McCLOUD
  Samuel 31
McCONNELL
  Alexander 36
McCUE
  Henry 29, 36, 40
McGAHAN
  Hugh 30
McGOULDRICK
  Peggy 29
McGUIRE
  James 34
McHENRY
  Ann 36
  James 36, 38
McKNIGHT
  William 34, 43
McMASTERS
  Charles J. 36
  Mary 37
McPHERSON
  Daniel 37
  Isaac 37
  Jonas 37
  Martha 37
McREA
  James 28
MEASE
  Robert 43
MENDENHALL
  William 37
MERTLAND
  John 38
  Susanna 38
MEZARVEY
  Thomas 43
MILAN
  James 44
MILLER
  Mordecai 28, 42
MILLS
  John 3
  William 35
MILNER
  William 34, 35
MITTCHELL
  Hugh 1
MOODY
  Samuel 38
  Thomas 38
MOORE
  Cleon 28
  George 38
MORRIS
  John 43
MOSS
  William 2, 26
MOXLEY
  William 38
MULLEN
  Patrick 38
  Thomas 38

MULLICHAN
  John 47
MUMFORD
  John 39
MURRAY
  Thomas 26
MYERS
  William 39

NEAL
  John 34
NEBLON
  James 39
NEVIN
  Duncan 34
NIVEN
  Duncan 1
NOUVOULET
  Jeane M. 39

OWENS
  William 39

PAGE
  William B. 31
PATON
  William 30
  Wm 44
Patowmack Company 4
PATTEN
  William 37
PATTON
  William 41
PELTON
  Enoch 35
PENDLE
  Thomas 39

PERRY
  Alexander 4
PETERKIN
  Thomas 37
PETTIT
  John 39
PEYTON
  Francis 43
POMERY
  William 31
PORTER
  Sarah 39
  Thomas 1, 11, 39, 43
Potomack Company 4
Potowmack Company 3
PRATT
  Margaret 39
PRICE
  Ellis 34
  Oliver 32
PUPPO
  Daniel C. 35

RAMSAY
  Dennis . 2, 34, 36, 39, 44, 45, 47
  John 39
  William 39, 40, 44, 45
REA
  John 36
REARDON
  John 28
REDMAN
  Sarah 40
  Thomas 32, 40
REINTZEL
  Andrew 41
REINTZELL
  Andrew 26
REYNOLDS
  John 28, 29, 41

Reynolds 30
Sarah 41
RICHARDS
   George 40
RICHTER
   John 36
RICK
   Christiana 41
   William 41
RICKARD
   William 28
RICKETTS
   John T. 42
RIDDLE
   Joshua 31
ROBERDEAU
   Daniel 1, 47
ROBERSON
   Matthew 2
ROBINSON
   Matthew 31, 36
   Sarah 41
ROGERSON
   Thos. 47
RUSSELL
   James 7, 10

SAUNDERS
   David 41, 42
   John 41
   Mary 41
   Peter 41, 42
   Sarah 41, 42
   Saunders 41
SCOTT
   Catherine iv
   Gustavus 4, 6
   James 4, 6
SHAKLE
   Dedrick 45

SHAW
   William 42
SHERUE
   Paul A. 39
SHREVE
   Benjamin 28, 41
SHROPSHIRE
   Eliza W. 42
   James 42
   John 42
   William 42
SHUCK
   Jacob 25
SIMMS
   Ch. 29
   Charles 2
SLACUM
   George . . 26, 30, 32, 33, 36, 42
SLADE
   Charles 1, 28
SLIMMER
   Christian 25
SLOAN
   Anna 42
   John 44
SMITH
   Alexander . . . 31, 32, 34, 36, 42
SMOOT
   Mr. 3
SPANGERBURGH
   Frederick 43
SPEARS
   Jerusha 35
STEEL
   William 30
STEIBER
   Michael 25, 32
STEUART
   John 10
   John A. 39
   Thomas 34

STEWART
  John 43
STIEBER
  Michael 40
STONE
  Robert 43
STUART
  James M. 43
SULLIVAN
  Elizabeth 43
  John 26
  Timothy 43
SUMMERS
  Elenor 43
  George 44
  Harvey 43, 44
  Isabel 43, 44
  Isabell 44
  Jane 43
  Lewis 44
  S. 44
  Thos. 44
  William . 1, 26, 30, 34, 38, 39, 42
                          -44, 47
SWANN
  Thomas 33
SWOPE
  Adam S. 25

TANDY
  Moses 40
TAYLOR
  George 26, 29, 36
  Jesse 32, 36, 39, 44
TEARNE
  Simon 45
TELEFRO
  Andrew 43
THOMAS
  John V. 35, 43

THOMPSON
  Jonah 11, 41
THORN
  Michael 27
THRELKELD
  John 4
TIBBS
  Willoughby 26
TRIDLE
  Fredrick 38
TUCKER
  Sarah 39, 40
  William 39, 40, 45
TURNER
  Charles 2, 28

VOWELL
  John 34
  John C. 33, 45
  Thomas 2, 34, 45

WALES
  Andrew 45
WANTON
  Philip 37, 38, 42
WARD
  William 26
WARDEN
  Ann 45
  William 45
WASHINGTON
  Bushrod 6, 9, 10
WATSON
  Josiah 37
WATTS
  John 38
WEIGHTMAN
  Richard 26, 35, 37

WEST
  Roger 45
  Thomas 29
WESTON
  Elizabeth 46
  John 46
  Lewis 27, 39, 46
  Mary 46, 47
  Polly 46
  Sally 46
  Sarah 46
WHEALEN
  Capt. 35
WHITING
  Mathew 6
  Thomas 6
WHITTREDGE
  Thomas 35
WISE
  John 25
  Peter . . . 10, 28, 30, 36, 39, 42
WOOLLS
  George 29
WORRELL
  Morris 32
WROE
  Absalom 47

YEATON
  William 1
YOST
  John 41
YOUNG
  James 36
YOUNGS
  George 33

www.ingramcontent.com/pod-product-compliance
Lightning Source LLC
Chambersburg PA
CBHW071753040426
42446CB00012B/2531